4-18-16

You Are The Boss!

Ralph,
Keep Hustling!
You'll be a millionaire!

Daniel A. Ally

Excerpt as permitted under the United States Copyright Act of 1976, no part of this publication may be reproduced and distributed in any form or by any means, or stored in a data base or retrieval system, without the prior written permission of the publisher.

You Are The Boss! Copyright © 2014 Daniel A. Ally
Printed and Manufactured in the United States of America.
All rights reserved.

Dignify Designs Publications
www.dignifydesigns.com
info@dignifydesigns.com

ISBN-10: 1495900495
ISBN-13: 978-1495900495

10 9 8 7 6 5 4 3 2 1

Table of Contents

Acknowledgments

This book is only possible with the support of my staff, family, friends, audience members, readers, and God Almighty.

This book is also dedicated to you.

You Are the Boss!

Special thanks to:

My committed father Chris

My dedicated mother Meena

My smart brother Jonathan

My creative sister Kirsten

And my best friend Shivanee

My Lord and Savior Jesus Christ

Foreword

Daniel,

When I met you four years ago, you were a completely different person. More recently in the last two years, there has been a deep transfiguration by which God has transcended you into His truth. It is astounding to see how far you have come on this miraculous journey. You have really traveled many miles to get where you are today!

Through your past experiences and life-altering conditions, I see a true man changing people's lives every day, not just for the better, but for the best. You are the resplendent light that liberates people as you delight them in sharing the truth about what freedom really means. Rather than falling into temptations of conforming to your peers, you have had the courage to research the greatest philosophers and provocative thinkers who ever lived.

Many times, I have seen what appeared to be immovable obstacles bestowed upon your path, but your robust appetite for learning has gravitated you to seek even more wisdom, faith, and truth to abolish the challenges that came before you. Even when there was a torrential downpour or ongoing blizzard, your audience could have relied on you driving four hours to deliver a free speech on a consistent basis. This is true devotion.

In this book, everyone can learn from his valuable lessons because of Daniel's deep insights. He has captured the true essence of leadership along with pure wisdom to assist you with your authority in professional and personal areas of your life. Be ready to inhale the truth, because this gladiator is full of character.

- Shivanee Patel

Initiation

You may be asking, “Why did you call this book ‘You are the Boss’?” I truly believe that you have everything within you to reach the apex of achievement. I believe that you have authority over your life and the capability to make decisions and go places that you never could have imagined. Many years ago, I realized that I had a greater potential for my life, but I ended up wasting many years as I listened to all of my naysayers. There were many people in my life who I let prevent me from going to where I needed to be, but I always felt sorry for them and continually felt that I needed in order to please them to gain their acceptance. At the time, I failed to acknowledge that there was a better plan for me and that I could become the man who I wanted to be with the proper guidance and understanding toward the journey of life.

All of the great philosophers agree that the major advantage in life is to 'know thyself'. Like me, it takes people several years to even know that they should know who they are. Knowing yourself will take a lifetime. No one really knows themselves entirely, no matter how much they think they do. It will take time to stretch and grow into the person you truly want to be, but before you get there, there is an abundance of information waiting to be discovered by you. I have read hundreds of books, talked to countless people, and traveled the world. I have learned so much in such a short time because I was willing and able to understand a few simple key principles that accelerated my life. I want to share these key principles with you.

The reason I wrote this book was because I know people need a philosophy. Everywhere we go, we assume some kind of structure, but how do we know it is right for us? How do we know that we are living lives of freedom? Do you really have the ability to explore all of your values in depth? These are some of the questions that will be answered in this book. Knowing yourself and your situation will be easily understood after the truth will be revealed to you.

This expository will outlay the precepts that have helped me build a fortified foundation. I believe that you can learn much from this book because I deliver the best that I know and I can assure you that you will find many treasures that will make your mind click into place. It's your decision how many of these gems you will invest upon and store for a rich future. Be aware that you will be stimulated on a different level of thinking. I will cover subjects such as time, power, relationships, money, sex, discipline, success, reading, thinking, communication, and so many other aspects that will assist you with your continuous development. It is a comprehensive book that offers interesting illustrations and concepts that you will instantly enjoy. You will want to read it over and over again because of the content it possesses. You are powerful and there are endless opportunities in front of you that you will soon be a part of. You need to know how to handle all of your ventures with passion and precision because YOU ARE THE BOSS!

1

The Land of Opportunity

"America is another name for opportunity".

-Ralph Waldo Emerson

My family came to America from Guyana when they were in their teens with an unsuspecting attitude that they will somehow fit in the unfathomable culture. Imagine walking on dirt roads and living in shacks while only eating chicken on holidays. The children would gather and share a bantam bowl of rice as the parents patiently wait to satiate upon the thoughts of 'maybe tomorrow I may eat'. Many of your ancestors have been in this situation as well. I don't want you to dwell on what seems to be generational despair. Those are not my intentions, because they were happy before they knew that there was a much better lifestyle. I will delight in having you conceive the opportunities that exist from a perspective that you may have previously reflected. I plan to show you a new resplendent light such as the first ones that glimmered to the unfamiliar eyes when they first came to New York City in the 1980's.

Like a virgin, I find myself in a world full of resources in that seem entirely unexplored. What is often radical to my mind is the lack of enthusiasm, perspective, and vision in our culture. It appears that most of the people in our society only work enough to keep their jobs, and seldom, little more. Why does this happen? As we wake up, the worries of the day infiltrate our minds, causing us to lose focus on what is really important, Almighty God. I came up with a thought a while ago that will enlighten you if you truly understand the original concepts that I will expound upon. Read this chapter scrupulously my dear friend.

It is perfectly logical to assume that a wise and competent Creator would provide for the needs of His creatures in their various stages of growth. People seem to lose focus on God because they find themselves in transient traps that keep them in their diurnal living. These are called 'cares of the world'. We feel that we must provide for our families, but like my family, we hold a mentality of scarcity. There doesn't seem to be enough to go around. Often times, we think of a God that is too small. In essence, we do not have faith at all in Him. But why do we think in such finite ways? He will certainly deliver when we do believe in Him. If fact, He wants to give us more than our finite minds can understand. The Giver is always free and ready to give.

"The smaller we are, the bigger our problems seem. The bigger we are, the smaller our problems seem." -Daniel Ally

Must we provide for our family the way we have pictured in our minds? When we dream of having a lot, but do not believe that is attainable, doesn't this hurt us? We see nice cars and houses, but do we believe that they are for us? Can we see ourselves living there, or do we delegate it to some other being that we may deem as more worthy or important than us? Don't we have imaginations that take us to various places? How many times do you shut your thoughts down? It seems like this kind of inferiority complex prevails in all levels of society, but why does it? Why do we feel like undeserving, despite all of the work we have invested in our whole lives? Do we trade dollars for hours and watch our dreams go by us as the years dwindle away?

It is because we are missing the real essence of life. There must be something bigger than us that can see everything. There seems to be some kind of omnipotent power that understands everything we do, because when we think a certain way, everything aligns to our thoughts. It seems like some mysterious force hears our thoughts and makes it happen just the way we expect it. Everything we expect seems to come to fruition, whether they are good or bad. I know for sure that the Living God exists. To be exact, He is the Boss!

Let's try another route. What about the things we possess? Do we buy what is on the market because that is what we want or do we buy what our neighbors buy? See, we often think that because other people are wearing certain clothes, partaking in reputable leisure, or cruising enjoyably, we feel that we must too. If not, we can always live vicariously through them as we build contempt in our hearts. This promulgates conformity, which hinders courage.

We then set our minds on established paths because we deem it worthy and successful. We 'go to school and get a job' because everyone is telling us to do it. Seldom do we think that there is an alternative lifestyle. These accepted journeys lead us to unimaginative lifestyles and places us in the inevitable boulevard of competition. We begin to do what everyone else is doing and compete in the markets that we think will give us the best results. This brings us emptiness at an all-time high. We commit psychological and spiritual suicide when we do not expect to get what we desire in our minds and hearts. The safest route is the most boring route.

Competition makes us stale because we do not compete for a prize that is ideal in our own minds and hearts. Competition engenders prizes that the people "think" they want, just because others have it. This creates a 'cookie cutter' mentality. Everyone wants to be cut out identically to the people they are surrounded by unless they know better and can think bigger. They settle for far less than they can attain just because they want acceptance from their peers. Men study sporting events and news seven days a week because that is what is trending on television, radio, and conversations at work, even when they know they could be doing something far greater. Women read gossip magazines, window shop, and watch adulterated reality television shows as their female counterparts bash men because they themselves have not been able to form any worthwhile relationships.

These are not appropriate studies for anyone. It is also not what we really want, but we think it appeals to others because they are conversant with the topics; therefore we become conversant in those topics too, even if we feel half-heartedly about them. Should we not be more careful of the media we deposit in our minds? Why put something in your mind if you do not fully believe in it? Why study something that will only get you to basic conversation? Why choose to be distracted? Distraction is a choice.

Essentially, you are searching for more substance, but it appears that no one around you has it and you settle for less because of the lack of truth in your life. You yearn to think bigger. Where can you find this depth? I will tell you soon. In the meanwhile, you should know that half-hearted living will create complacency, which is the enemy of excellence.

This misconduct of complacency brings no excitement to your life and enthusiasm is dramatically curtailed. Our slothful lifestyle would make our forefathers, writers, poets, philosophers, teachers, and business pioneers weep maniacally. As mentioned earlier, we create spiritual suicide when we do not live the life that God designed for us live. You can call it the "inner voice" or the "Higher Power" if God is too serious of a word for you. When we do not get the life we want, we create excuses. We keep finding all the ways to escape the life that God has created for us. We tend to think we are bigger than Him.

Basically, our attention is competing with everything that is irrelevant to what we should really be thinking about. We major on minors. We then begin to make excuses upon why we are not getting the results that we want in life. Life is the study of where our attention goes. It is about becoming who we are. All excuses come from the indecision to execute your lifetime goals. It begins as soon as someone begins to feel inferior about themselves or their position. Every time you hear someone make excuses, run as far as possible, because that person is unhappy and will try to bring you down—like the crabs tearing down other crabs in a barrel. It's time for you to escape that terrible barrel of death. The best way is to avoid mass conformity in its entirety.

Could it be possible that a person has most of what they have because other people have it as well? We try to achieve levels of success that will advance our social position. We begin to conform because of our inability to think about ways in which we can create a worthwhile lifestyle that thrives with our individualism. We compromise our values everyday so that we can have food on our tables. A man thinks to himself, "A little dishonesty will help my family!" Little does he know that this will catch up to him in the long-run. Conformity allows us to step down from our best for the sake of acceptance. It makes us desperate to please others, but while the others aren't looking, we tend to hate and resent ourselves and the people whom we seek to please because of our inability to escape the mess we created. We lower our standards substantially when we commit to conformity. Stop conforming, start performing!

Undoubtedly, we must conform in some ways, but we should also consider creating. You are allowed to create what you want. Why do you not? Is it because you surround yourself with imitators and non-creators? This world is full of people who conform. People want to run in the direction as everyone else because they believe that it is safe. As soon as they start to turn away from what everyone else is doing, life begins to bring challenges that most people do not think they can handle. Why would you give up working for an employer if they are giving you a decent living, good benefits, a nice phone and car? After all, you only have to be a slave who is subjected for 40-60 hours a week? Isn't it worth it? Forget that! You can create a different lifestyle for yourself. You don't have to be fed by an owner. You are not an animal. You are the Boss! Just wait until you finish this book.

"All things are difficult before they are easy."
-Thomas Fuller

You may be asking, why don't people not create the lifestyle that they want? The answer is really simple. I hear people talking about how we put limitations on our minds as they recite clichés to gain approval. "The Only Thing We Have to Fear Is Fear Itself", they say, to win approval of the audience who lives in fear. Of course people will agree to the platitude, who would not? This is not a knock to Franklin Delano Roosevelt, a resolute leader of our great country; it is more of an admonishment to the proud emulators who live banal lives. Why do they? It is exactly where I want to take you. Look at the first question of this paragraph–now here in the answer: People fear criticism. They do not create because people will judge their ideas and their work. It may not be deemed 'worthy'. They are also afraid to fail. For centuries, people have not done what they know they should do because of what other people think about them. We let the thoughts of others stop us from listening to the call of excellence in our lives. We limit ourselves and miss out on all of the great opportunities we should, could, and would have taken. Our ships will pass by many times during the course of our lives, but then when it is too late, we utter the words, "Shoulda, Coulda, Woulda."

The disparity of not doing what we know we should has been in existence since the beginning of humankind and it is not easily understood. Most people do not even make a serious attempt to serve their purpose in this world because they have 'voices in their heads' that tell them that if they fail, everyone will make fun of them. This voice might have developed for you at a young ago because children would laugh at you every time you made a mistake. In short, you have been criticized because of your mistakes and failures. Since we are social creatures, we tippy-toe around life because we seek constant approval from those in which we interact. The last thing we want to do is feel rejected.

We carry this fear of criticism, failure, and rejection all the way to our adulthoods, but we are often too afraid to admit it because of our false sense of pride. We then begin to compete for things that do not even matter. We try to attain things that were not even made for us. We become unnatural when we begin to compete. Our thoughts become smaller and smaller as we participate in the monotony and dissipate our consciousness of reality.

It causes immense distress to find people living exclusively for the acceptance by their "competitors." To explicate further, I know of a woman who wears top-notch clothing to make her 'enemies' or 'competitors' feel jealous. Have you seen this pattern before? What about the man who buys a brand new BMW because he thinks that makes him feel important among his equally struggling peers? This causes no love, which invites no God, because the material substance is born out of pride. Pride is the greatest destroyer of the human soul.

Many people have a complete emptiness in their souls that no amount of consumerism can void. They live lives of quiet desperation, as Henry David Thoreau once said. They think that their 'things' will cover the emptiness in their lives, especially when they show off to their competitors. I have a beautiful Mercedes-Benz, and I got that in the process of delivering immaculate service from creating a purposeful lifestyle through enriching the lives of others.

"Competition is a sin." - John D. Rockefeller

Pride deeply affects the ostentatious person and those who are envious equally. One may not agree, and you are obliged to your own theory, but this actually depreciates the human race. How does this work? Both types of people lose self-esteem by one-upping each other and never admitting the deep, heart-splitting pains of competition, or mass conformity. When this happens, we feel utterly worthless because we know we want to have pity on each other. How can we have pity for others when we don't even have pity for ourselves? This unforgiving attitude creates a superficial relationship not only between each other, but within us. This conflict is called cognitive dissonance. An example of this could be like a person who teaches people how to get out of debt, but is living in debt the whole time he renders his lessons. How can you admit the truth to someone you think that you are better than, if you think you are better than you know you actually are?

Behind the scenes, these people inflict deep wounds upon themselves. They curse their families, binge drink on the weekends, and resort to pornography. Although I could not list all the infractions of the soul, these are the primary ones in which my clients have entrusted me with to share publicly. Why all the unnecessary pain? It appears that when we are indebted to people and cannot pay the love that is due, we hurt ourselves in the process. Sometimes we hate ourselves so much that we partake in destructive behaviors when no one is looking. This is all because of competition.

If you consider antiquity for a moment, undisciplined people would take loans with all the right intentions to pay, however they may resort to self-deprecation if they weren't able to pay the exorbitantly accrued debt. It is the same in the modern world. People do not kill themselves, but they cover themselves in tattoos, piercings, and incessantly celebrate curse words as they evade truth to justify their unfortunate disposition. Does this answer your questions? Face yourself and embrace the truth about who you are. We need each other because love is the veritable components of our interdependencies. Here is a question to ponder: Since we were made in the image of God and God does not compete, why should we compete if we are just like Him?

Knowing God will give you the life-changing capacity to create that which can enhance the lives of many others as well as yourself. You will not compete with others because you will understand its detrimental effects. I believe Christianity is the most extraordinary adventure for anyone. Anyone can become a Christian by reading Christian texts and the Bible. It will open up doors that you never even knew existed. This is not about religion, rituals, and rigidness, but more about having a real relationship with the all-inspiring God and his Son Jesus Christ. Being a Christian has turned my life around completely and has taken me places where I never thought I could go. I promise you that it will help you change your life as well. Remember, You Are the Boss!

2

Thoughts and Imagination

"There is nothing either good or bad, but thinking makes it so."
— William Shakespeare

My life was forever changed in the June of 2012 when I heard the audio recording called "The Strangest Secret" by Earl Nightingale. In only six words, Earl Nightingale expounds his wisdom in dramatic fashion by saying "we become what we think about." I was so surprised to realize that my thoughts were really holding me back at that time and up until that point, I decided to do something about it.

Immediately, I wanted to learn how I could help construct my mind to focus on what was really important, instead of thinking about women, food, and sports, which were the majority of my thoughts. I knew there was more to life than those thoughts. I was then committed to re-engineering my entire belief system. My life started to work out perfectly after I really understood what Earl Nightingale was saying. Thinking really does make a difference in our lives. Our thoughts determine how we act.

Metacognition has become a hobby of mine. This is where you find yourself thinking about thinking. You must always position yourself and schedule time to think. Too often, people think about their vacations fifty weeks in a year, and then when they take their two weeks, they are thinking about their work during their vacation. Thinking needs the proper time and place. Thinking must be organized. It must be understood in order to do it properly. Thinking is a very challenging way of life because it requires mental exertion and facing reality on a daily basis while managing to keep your sanity. Thinking makes you completely whole and it is useful as long as you decide that you are going to take control of your life. Thinking takes a lot of time and is demanding of your mind but it is worth it when you make better decisions because of the thought that you put into it.

Did you know that every material good around you is composed of the thoughts other people? Everything around you has been created by an organized and specifically directed thought process! All things were created through the daily habits of applied thinking. Everything that has been made was a deliberate idea that was put into action by someone else. Because of your thoughts, things can be created. This means that your imagination comes from your thoughts and can manufacture anything you create in it as long as you believe in it and take action upon it. Every product and service has been created by someone who learned how to think.

All of your exceptional ideas should be stored in your journal (I will talk more about journaling later). All of your ideas should be regarded with the utmost value. No one should put their ideas to waste, even if they may sound impossible or unrealistic at first. We all get at least 2-5 ideas per day that could change our lives if only we would put them into action. Many of our ideas can help us breakthrough in life and expand innovatively. Most people do not put their ideas to the test because they are afraid of their own minds and the amount of power that it actually possesses. Again, as the first chapter indicated, they are also afraid of the criticism that they may receive. They have F.E.A.R., which stands for 'False Evidence Appearing Real.' They fear that their ideas won't be accepted when expostulated, so they avoid the business of thinking.

Most of the time, we are not surrounded with people who would want to hear or understand our ideas. In a way, we expect our ideas to get shot down. We even prevent discussing our ideas because of this fear. This apprehension makes us suppress what is really in our minds, which can diminish our souls to its diminutive existence causing us to go to our graves completely unfulfilled. We can only feel complete once we act upon our ideas to reach our desires.

Can you believe that most people are afraid of their own thoughts? They know that their minds are powerful that they are afraid to use it because of what others may think about them. For example, let us use a fictitious character named Bryan. Bryan is an amazing, undiscovered opera singer at age thirty, but because he had a family of five since a young age, he had to drop out of high school his senior year and has been working at a factory for the last twelve years to support them. He will not pursue his dreams of being an opera singer to the test due to several reasons.

Firstly, he will think that it is too late to start a musical career. Since he didn't go to college, he might say to himself, "college is too hard" or "only smart people go to college." He may also tell everyone, "I am trying to get into music school," but this is only to test their responses for a sign of approval. He will receive sensation if their responses are positive. He will not actually believe in himself because their affirmations will suffice in his heart.

Another way in which he will limit his thoughts of being an opera singer is by knowing, secretly, that no one in the factory will support his thoughts because they are not like-minded and supportive of a talented opera singer. He will conform to their ways, but never go his own route because of his self-imposed limitations. He will continue to make excuses as he ages, but never admit that it was totally his fault and no one else's. He may even start blaming his wife, family, his former school, the government, his job, taxes, and everyone else, including a long list of everyone who "held him back."

Furthermore, if his wife doesn't support him, he will be too concerned about pleasing her immediate needs. He will assume that he is no longer a potential opera singer after she nags him about the smallest things in life. His big picture of being an opera singer will evaporate because of his inability to express himself by using his natural gifts. All of this happened because he did not take the time to think internally and communicate externally to people who could help him become an opera singer. He suppressed his thoughts to please the people around him, but he never took the time to see what was actually in his own heart. In a way, familiarity breeds contempt because he can become frustrated in his internal insanity of not being able to do that which is deemed different. Since he cannot express himself in his own natural ways as an opera singer, this makes him hold a contemptuous attitude unless he finds another way to channel his internal frustrations. This underdeveloped man named Bryan is not the only one in the world who suffers this abuse. There are billions of people who have been through this tragedy of life. That is, the inability to produce useful and productive thoughts.

Did you know that you can organize your mind in the same way you organize your house, car, or desk? Often times our thoughts run rampant, which can lead us to ponder ideas that we know we should not be thinking of. Like Bryan, we could easily shut down our real desires to please others. You must prioritize your thoughts and make them real as you set goals and standards for yourself. You must execute your plans as you think through thoroughly of all your options. I will cover more on this in the subsequent chapters. Finding the right people is imperative when trying to help manifest those thoughts and know that it takes time for them to come to fruition. Many times, we do not even know where to start. Everything starts in our minds, at the impulses of our thoughts.

Most of us have amazing imaginations that we are afraid to use. When we do use our imagination, it is mostly some form of an unrelated, reoccurring fantasy that will never happen. We often build an empire in our minds regarding everything that may be irrelevant to our success, even if it is silly to our world. For instance, many business men are thinking about golf when they should be focusing on 'the big contract' that they are working on. Their bodies are in one place, but their minds are in another entity. Females in college may be thinking about their boyfriends that they hope to marry as they listen to their math professor go over calculus problems. They are picturing the wedding, the limousine, the kiss at the altar, their parents, the wedding cake, and everything else unrelated to the reality of being in calculus class.

What if these people focused on one thing at a time? Do you ever go in the shower, roll around in bed, or drive in the car and you are thinking about everything besides that present moment? Your mind escapes you and takes you into certain peculiar moments or 'daydreams' of thought. You need to concentrate on what is really important and never major on minor distractions. Get down to business and put full thought into your work. Command your attention to your present moment and focus on the task at hand. Take everything slowly. Every master was once a disaster. Think about how you can be better at what you are doing.

Nothing great was accomplished without blood, sweat, tears, and years of toil. When your mind starts to wander, get it back to where it needs to be. You must have dominion over your thoughts and imagination. Thinking time will come at the right moments of deliberate reflection. After all, you can control your thoughts because you are the boss!

"A journey of a thousand miles begins with a single step."

-Lao-Tzu

Our man, Bryan, is destined to be an opera singer, but he may also be distracted by his factory work, instead of focusing on how he can become the finest opera singer. He never trained his mind to escape the daily hardships and focus on something more ideal. He never realized that he could still do his work, but still have pleasure in chasing his dreams as an opera singer. It may be difficult to use your imagination and fantasize about what you actually want when life brings its daily challenges. In Bryan's case, it would be a good idea to think about being an opera singer while he is working a job that he has already mastered. Of course, thinking about it and imagining something worthwhile is good, but he needs to take appropriate action too.

Sometimes it is challenging to come back to reality unless your mind is trained. Your fears can easily become bigger than your dreams and trap you into what is called 'FUDs'-Fears, Uncertainty, and Doubts. Once the 'FUDs' settle in, they will be difficult to uproot. They are the great disablers of the mind. That is why there are many discontent people in this world. They are unable to get the FUDs out of their minds. They are trapped in a self-made prison. You must always keep dominion over your mind and protect anything that may enter into it. When you are watching what you think, you will be thinking about what you watch. You will be able to focus on what is really important, making your dream a reality.

"Our doubts are traitors, and make us lose the good we oft might win, by fearing to attempt." -William Shakespeare

As I travel to different areas, I realize more and more that we can easily become a product of our environment. Everyone around us affects the way we think; no matter how much we try to avoid it.

Some people say, "No matter where I go, I can turn down other peoples' influence" or "no one can make me think differently." I tried to believe this theory for a while, and I realized that it is impossible not to be influenced by the area where you work, live, and play. The thoughts of others will always impact the way we think because we will always be reacting to them, consciously or unconsciously.

As I was raised in inner New York City, I never knew how much influence the city had until after I revisited. It really surprised me when I observed the people in the lower-income areas. I talked to them about various common topics. They could not see the trap they lived in. They did not understand why welfare is not the best plan for them. It seemed perfectly fine that they could live and eat for free without work and minimal contribution. Little did they know about the endless opportunities that were waiting their discovery. They failed to reason about how they could partake in opportunities outside their everyday and unstable conditions.

They could not think outside of the environment of the city in which they lived, worked, and played. I thought to myself, "Why can they not see?" It boggled my mind that they were allowing their thoughts to be blocked by the thoughts of others and the circumstances of everyday living. It seemed like they were quite content with their lifestyles.

The people in the ghettos could not see a reason to eat healthy, exercise regularly, or place themselves in a position where they could be around people smarter than they are. They did not see the value of reading and learning, nor did they understand the process of thought. They underestimated the value of time and money. They laughed at me when I told them I operated by schedules and deadlines. They could not see why living in a 'concrete jungle' was not good and could not foster their growth. They did not recognize why plants and trees are essential for breathing. It didn't make sense to not litter in the streets because "it's not their fault if there is trash on the streets," "I won't get in 'trouble' for it", or "everyone else does it". Some of the men could not understand that they could be successful without living the street life that consisted of hustling drugs, getting into the music industry, living a life of crime, or playing some kind of ball (football, basketball, baseball, etc.).

They found themselves in a trap and because that is what they know, that is all they thought they were capable of. Deep inside, I believe they really knew their circumstances, but believed that they could not do anything about it because of the people they were surrounded by. Even though they blamed an exterior force like the government, they knew innately that it was really their fault for not being able to escape the trap that they were so unfortunate to inherit. In essence, living in the ghettos is all they ever expected out of life and not much more. They lacked the vision because they lacked the inability to process reality by the means of thinking.

"Without a vision, the people perish."- Jesus Christ

I understand today how thankful I am to escape the trap that may not easily be identified. It is very subtle and cannot be seen unless you get out of it or hear a different perspective. It would take years to recognize it if you remained in it. Many people can only see the trees, but cannot see the forest. Their visions are myopic, instead of being panoramic. After all, they do believe that there is very little to hope for. If your mindset is, "only certain people get the good life" or "you need to do 'certain things' to get there", how can you be able to think the way you need to in order to get to where you need to be?

What good can you do with where you live and what little opportunity you think you have. You need to constantly be working on your ways of thinking and the kind of lifestyle that is actually available to you. It will amaze you once you start a new way of thinking. Your imagination will steer you into directions you could have never dreamed of. If you are going to think, you might as well think big.

I ran into a young homeless man in his mid-twenties while I visited Washington D.C. He pleaded me for only three pennies. He really did a good job selling it to me, and I wondered, "Why doesn't this man assume a more worthwhile career than begging and burdening people?" I asked him if begging was the best he thought that

he could do and he told me, "This is all people are willing to give me". I told him that he needed to take initiative and learn how to give value to people, instead of begging and burdening for so little money.

He said he didn't know where to start, and then I pointed across the street to where the Dr. Martin Luther King Jr. Library was. He said, "Why are you pointing there?" I told him, "You need to start thinking of ways to make a living because you have a potential in sales once you clean yourself up". He told me that it would take too much time to do all the studying and learning to live the life he wanted to live. The immediate reward of three pennies seemed to be more of a priority to him. I asked him, "Do you see yourself doing this for the next forty years?" He answered, "This is what fate dealt me".

He really believed in his thoughts and imagination that begging and burdening was the best he could do. He was unwilling to feed his mind, even with one of the best libraries that offered free services. The library had all of the answers that he could have thought of, if not more. He had everything he needed to become a millionaire in the next ten years, except for a proper mindset. He is failing at life and knows it because he will not dare to assume that he can do better. Is this not the same way of thinking for many of us in America and across the globe? Do we take for granted this incredible vessel of the mind which is often going to waste?

It's easy for some of us to live in the suburbs and drive luxury cars without thinking about the atrocities of the majority of people who live urban lives. Conversely, it is also easy for some of us to sit in the cities and think about how 'perfect' a life in the suburb would be, even though we may never think it is attainable in our lifetimes. However, you must think about how you can render service by cooking up a formula with your thoughts as the recipe. If you make a concoction that envelops yourself only around what is important, you will truly succeed. You need to build a success system that never fails by applying what you know is right and link it with action.

If you live in the suburbs, you can help the people in the city to believe that they could make it to the suburbs. If you live in the city, you can start to believe that a life in the suburbs is possible. Either way, it all starts with the renewal of your thoughts. Also, if you're already located in the area in which you dream of living extravagantly, then go out and explore all of the possibilities. Socialize with people you wouldn't normally surround yourself with and you will discern a whole new perspective.

"Poverty is the worst form of violence." - Mahatma Gandhi

You must think things through thoroughly. Like Bryan, our fictitious character, most people do not think enough. They are distracted by everything else going on in their lives. They marvel at the pulse of ever interruption, never getting the chance to focus on one specific task for a solid period of time. Then, there are the people who become too excited once they receive a thought on impulse. Some people act too irrationally upon their thoughts. There is a specific reason why more than 80% of American businesses fail. A person who gets ideas and start businesses too quickly without proper planning is sure to fail. They haven't thought about all of the consequences and the seasons of life. There are all sorts of trends and outliers we must consider in the journey of living.

Many people fail to seek the proper advice or work around real professionals. Instead they choose to fly solo or work with amateurs. Others have too much pride to do research and passionately dive into an empty pool because they thought that it was filled with water. They settle for amateur work because they are unable to think everything through. They neglect to 'tie up to loose ends' or finish what they started.

A great example of this is the amount of people who want to become professional speakers. There are many people want to be professional speakers because it looks easy. They think it will be something that is lucrative because they see other successful people doing it. Many of them fail to count the costs associated, which are many. It sometimes seems that many have the wrong motives for doing it. There are many ways that people fail in the industry of professional speaking (see if these relate to your profession too):

Here are a few:

- Inability to recognize their target audience
- Unwillingness to practice
- Unwillingness to travel or work weekends (they don't realize that many programs are held on the weekends)
- Inability to walk away from a secure job to a lifestyle that is less secure
- Lack of leadership skills
- Unwilling and able to give hundreds of free speeches

- Unwillingness to invest in themselves by attending seminars, reading various books, learning critical business skills, and connecting with meeting planners and colleagues
- Poor choice of wardrobe
- Underestimation of actual work involved as a professional speaker
- Lack of support from people in their lives
- Lack of patience
- No marketing and promotion such as online and offline promotional strategies
- Lack of extensive research on companies
- Lack of time-management skills
- Lack of real-world and business experience to deal with people effectively
- Inability to sell their expertise, assuming that they have one
- Forgetting to ask crucial questions
- Lack of knowledge on their topic or area of expertise
- Complete neglect of products that disservice their audiences

- Lack of confidence to get up and speak when they need to, at-will
- Lack of business awareness
- Lack of communication skills (Imagine that!)

Like any industry, there are also many other nuances in professional speaking such as: mechanics, stage movement, acting, adult learning theories, spontaneity, gestures, vocal variety, facial expressions, breathing, humor, physical appearance, event distractions, phone usage, voice projection, conviction, adlibbing, and many more that I could write another book about it if I were to continue this list.

All I am saying is that diligence is due. Once you get a thought, it may be an excellent idea, especially if you pursue it. Your idea could be worthwhile if it relates to your priorities. Be sure to time your idea perfectly. Mistiming a perfect idea can be a major blunder and mislead you into believing that it was never good to begin with. Sometimes, the timing is not right to act on the idea at that moment. That is why your ideas must be stored. Thoughts manifest themselves and will materialize if dwelt upon long enough. Your desires exist they must come to fruition. Is there a place you want to go? A person you want to be? I person you want to meet? Go after it aggressively with a well-constructed plan.

My father used to say, “don’t get too excited and jump into an empty pool.” Every time I disobeyed that command, there was a consequence that could have mitigated if I had only heeded that simple advice. I realized that I needed to think before I jumped into any more opportunities. I began to study at length and made sure I understood what I was getting into.

"We cannot solve our problems with the same thinking we used when we created them."
-Albert Einstein

The reason why most people do not think thoroughly is because it requires a lot of effort. We live in a world filled with people who seek instant gratification. Why think when you can simply 'Google it?' They want everything as fast as possible and if there are moments to spare, thinking becomes very belaboring. Instead, many people suppress their thoughts with television, music, or some other form of leisure, only to find that they will be bored with it in due time. By the time they realize that their challenge gets worse, they either stop the procrastination and deal with the problem or let it torment them until they become agonizing and deleterious to their lifestyle.

It is surprising how many people are willing to let their trashcan pile up when they can simply pull the bag out, draw the strings, and dispose of the trash—all in one minute or less. It is the same with the mind. We can easily take care of what is piling up and hurting us. Some people will venture to eat cold leftovers just because they are too lazy to put it in the microwave for one minute. One time, I saw someone sacrifice the pleasure of eating a bowl of cereal just because they were too lazy to walk into another room and get a spoon. They settled the score by picking at it and letting the cereal get soggy, despite the constant complaining of being hungry. People take pills when they know their headaches could be gone in a few hours. They are also willing to take a shot or two of liquor to sedate themselves if they are fidgeting and cannot get to bed at night. Our society largely settles for anything that provides the quickest fix and least amount of thought.

We live in a society of people who complain all the time. You could go to the mall, gym, or any public place and will hear all kinds of people complaining. I see men and women at the gym complaining all the time about how they are out of shape when they could be working out. I once heard a woman complaining to a clerk at a department store about her shopping habit as he continued to sell her things she said she could not afford. I heard a man complain to his friend at the supermarket about how he couldn't stay away from the bleu cheese while he was tossing a half-dozen bottles in his cart for the Super Bowl game at his house. Complaining destroys our creativity and thought processes. We lose imagination because we are so focused on what is wrong instead of what is right with the situation. We lose valuable time and miss out on great opportunities when we complain.

The world we live in contains people who say they will do something, but never end up doing it. If a man were to say that he 'promises' to show up for a meeting, but when the time comes, he is nowhere to be found. This disparity of 'talking, but not walking' is not new, for it has been in existence to humankind for thousands of years. Many a man has said he would do something, but never executed. This causes upset for the people that they let down, which in turn, will be reciprocated by the person who was offended.

We can find all kinds of good people who do not show up for their assignments. Attendance everywhere is at an all-time low because our leaders are refusing to show up at the right times. This leaves you room to lead, especially if you notice people are not showing up. Leadership is always in demand and you should take you chance to be the boss every moment you get, even though no one has asked you to do it. When you do it, they will appreciate you.

People get mad when they feel entitled to something, but do not receive it. They take their hostility out on innocent victims because they haven't taken the time to think about why things are the way they are. People also complain because this of a symptom of their impatience and inability to take a few moments to think about why they are living, what they are doing, and also why they are complaining. "Why am I not getting what I deserve?" some may ask. They do not realize that the old stove will start once they put wood in it and light it on fire. Education can help you understand why humankind cannot reach a higher level of thinking. Wisdom is available to everyone who seeks it. It is the most valuable commodity that you can have, because you can only gain from it and no one can ever take it away from you.

To change your approach about thinking and your behavior, stay away from defeated people at all costs. If you hang out with someone who complains, you will most likely start complaining too. If you hang out with someone who is thankful and full of praise, you will be thankful and full of praise too. If you hang out with the fools, you will be a fool. When you hang out with the wise people, you will be wise. You will find an adjustment in mentality in both scenarios. Do not surround yourself with the impatient, vulgar, or violent persons, even if they are in your family. Your mind operates on anything you feed it, whether if it is good or bad, it does not discriminate. It only does what you command it to do. If it was not true, your cognition would have told you so. My Mother was right when she told me early on in life "you are who your friends are." Thanks Mother!!

It is your duty to feed your mind the proper nutritional meal of knowledge necessary to attain the path that you have chosen. Do not live your life mindlessly and be controlled by people who have an agenda for you. True authority requires you to know who you are, what you represent, and where you want to be. It also requires the proper mindset and the inspiration to take each day at a time. I recommend that you read at least one inspirational book per month to maintain the right attitude. It will change your world and motivate you to the next level. Be careful not to get addicted to reading the easy books, for you may not reap results and it will become mental candy as your mind could rot from it with excessive indulgence. I met a man who read six self-help books a month and it was still unfortunate that he still could not help himself because he was always thinking about the next book he could get his hands on without setting any kind of goals or action plans. Read a few inspirational books per year. To keep things interesting, mix them up with applicable information for the advancement of your career. You will also want to have knowledge on various subjects. You will find that your thoughts and imagination will go very far and you will be able to develop an indomitable will to achieve anything you plan to undertake.

Society is bombarded with non-sense and impending danger from all kinds of directions. Pretend that your mind is a garden that you must cultivate. First, start with the right kind of soil and climate (environment). You can't plant tomatoes in bad soil, nor will it grow in a cold region like Alaska. Then, you must choose the right kind of seed (your dream or goal). Next, water that seed (your action plan and strategy). Next, you must give it time (deadline of your goal or dream). In the right season, you will be able to produce the fruit that you have expected. Moreover, you must keep producing and create other plants in your farm when you become more ambitious. When you reach a certain point, you can show others how to do it, which is the best part!

"3 Stages in Life - Earning, Learning, and Returning."
-Anonymous

Let me give you an example. If you had a dream or goal of becoming a prominent real estate agent for luxury homes, and you are surrounded in an inner city as I mentioned earlier, you will first need to locate fertile ground. You may need to start by locating the proper firm that you can work with. This will be the soil.

Assuming that you are qualified for the position with the right credentials, you must read at least 5-10 books on sales, real estate, and business skills. This will be you watering the seed. You must be able to stick with your plan so that you begin to produce fruit. When you begin producing fruit, you can leverage your profit and service by building your own firm and showing others how you did it. Now you are able to build your own garden because you have a crop of plants and fruits. At last, you can teach others how to replicate your business model, which is the most rewarding thing you can do to yourself and your fellow citizen.

Make sure you realize that this started with the right environment and the original seed. Changing either the environment or the seed may be risky and rewarding. For instance, let's say you wanted to start a yacht company in Florida. The yacht is a different seed and the location, which is Florida, is a different environment. It may only be profitable if you know what you are doing and you have someone else who can help you cultivate your garden. Give your garden room and time to grow. With the proper resources, plans, and assistance, you can attain any kind of garden that you want. Ensure that your garden gets the proper nutrients to grow into what you planned it to be.

Your imagination is infinite and can take you anywhere you choose to go. Imagination is the art of seeing things invisible. You have an incredible imagination. It only needs to be specialized and intelligently directed to a specific purpose. Your thoughts are very powerful and will put you in whichever place you direct it. You have the choice to think in any way that you want. Konrad Adenauer said,

"We all love under the same sky, but we don't all have the same horizon." Many people are on different levels, you just have to choose which level you want to be on. You have this choice within your reach. Everything begins with thoughts and imagination. Will you
begin to think about what is really important? You can refine your authority by having dominion over your thoughts and imagination. You are the Boss!

"Reach high, for stars lie hidden in your soul. Dream deep, for every dream precedes the goal." - Pamela Vaull Starr

3

Questions

"Judge a man by his questions rather than his answers."

– Voltaire

Aren't questions extremely important? No one can go on for a day around people without hearing someone ask them a question. If no one asks a question, the person will ask themselves a question. While I was taking a test in college, it appeared that I had been answering questions my whole entire life. I wondered, "Why does everyone ask questions and why do I need to give them the answer that they want?" My curiosity began with a question. The professors were asking questions. Your parents ask you questions. The doctor asks you questions. Your boss asks you questions. The best sales people in the world ask questions before they are able to serve you the best way possible. It seems like when the proper question is asked, the right answer usually comes along.

I also realized that most people are searching for answers in life. Everyone is saying, "I wish I knew what to do" or "I would like to know the answer to that one," but it seems like when you search for answers, you do not get the chance to ask questions. It seems like the uneducated keeps supplying the answers, while the wise keeps demanding the questions. People consistently fail to ask questions, even if they do, they do not ask the right questions. Remember when you teacher used to say to the class, “There is no such thing as a bad question?”

Here are some uneducated questions:

Many times people ask the question, “What did I do wrong?” A better question would be, “What can I do better?”, “What did I do right?”, or “How can I improve my performance for next time?”

People frequently ask, “What is wrong with you?” The better question would be, “What do you need?”, “Is everything okay?”, “What can I do for you?”, or “How can I help you?”

Some will ask, “Isn’t that expensive?” The better question will be “How much does that cost?” “Do you have a payment option for this car?” or “What is the price of that particular house?”

They also are used to express incredulity or assume answers in their questions by asking: “Didn’t the bigger guy win the fight last night?” The better question would be, “Who won the fight last night?” or “How did the match go last night?” Another one of these questions could be, “The museum is three blocks up right?” A better question would be, “Where is the museum?”

Then, there are disapproval questions such as, "Aren't you going to help me or are you just going to sit there and watch me do this all by myself?” This question appears as though the person feels obligated, even if they do not want to help. It is very negative and resentful. A better question could be, “Can you please give me a hand?” or “I will buy you a dinner if you help me out, okay?”

"Don't you want something to drink?" This is a question that seems like the person who is being asked will reject the drink before it is even offered. Instead, try "What can I get you to drink?", "Are you thirsty?", or "Would you like water or lemonade?"

"Isn't she going to come?" This expresses doubt. It seems like the person who is asking the question doesn't believe that the person they are waiting for will ever come. A better question would be, "What time did she say she was coming again?" or "When is she going to be here?"

"Don't you have to go to school today?" This person is asking a question, but is ready to tell the person off and show them why they are right and why the person they are questioning is wrong. Any question posed as an "I am right and you are wrong" is a bad question. Never set people up for failure in your questions, instead, let them succeed. Go for 'what' is right, not 'who' is right. You can ask that question in a different way, "What time do you have to go to school today?" or "Are you ready for school today?"

Questions must be more specific. Many people have the right ideas, but the wrong approach. Some will ask incomplete and vague questions such as, "Can you get the paper?" The better question will be "Can you get your birth certificate on the desk next to the computer in my room?" Some people who ask for directions in the city will ask, "Where is a good restaurant?" versus "I am looking for a very high-class Italian restaurant in the area, can you direct me to one?" Specificity builds credibility. The person will be able to understand the question much more if you are specific.

"A wise man can learn more from a foolish question than a fool can learn from a wise answer."- Bruce Lee

Questions should be in a proper tone of voice. When your mother asks, "Did you get the bread at the supermarket?" she could ask in various ways. She could ask it as though she assumed you did not get the bread at the supermarket. In her mind she would assume, "He never gets the bread even though I ask him every time." She could ask the question in a way that sounds doubtful as she worries, "If he doesn't get the bread, what should I do? Let me make sure I ask him first." She can ask in a joking way, and think "I know he is irresponsible and I will forgive him if he forgets the bread". She can ask in a regular way and think "Now I am not going to assume whether you have the bread or not, therefore I am going to ask you as if I really needed to know." From this, you can see that there are many ways for mother to see if you got her the bread.

There are also pre-suppositional or loaded questions, such as "Have you stopped beating your wife?" or "Did you waste all your money on the lottery again?" This may be used as a joke or to embarrass an audience or person, because any answer a person could give would imply more information than he was willing to affirm. This could also be a sarcastic question. I recommend avoiding these kinds of questions. Sometimes people are offended, but it is usually a tease among good friends. It can create hostility if it backfires. It is better to be safe and not ask these kinds of questions.

Questions should be either open ended or close ended. An open ended question is, "What did you think of the movie?" This allows the person to formulate a response as long as they want to. This is a great way to learn about who you are dealing with. The person will tell you as much as they think you need to know. Then, there are close ended questions such as “Do you like black cars?” These questions are used to find a quick answer in just one word, yes or no. Both questions are important and if you can master them, you can get anywhere you want to go. The mastery of questions is the beginning of persuasion.

There are also tag questions, which are structured in a way to get the questioner to make a declarative statement or an imperative and is turned into a question by adding an interrogative fragment (the "tag"), such as right in "You remembered the eggs, right?", or “You are good at this, aren’t you?”, and "It's cold today, isn't it?" Tag questions can be answered with a yes or no. They can also start a conversation or keep things very brief. They are very good sales questions to win the rapport of the client.

There are also “either/or”, “rather questions” or “this/that” questions. They are questions like, “Do you like black or white?”, “Is he slim or fat?”, “Would you rather be the fastest person in the world or the strongest person in the world?” These questions are designed to get a one word response. They are meant to keep things moving. They also allow the person being asked the question to think about what they prefer or what they may possibly want. These are also great sales questions.

Since we are talking about questions, “when/if” questions really matter. For instance, when someone asks another person a question, they could ask it like this: “If you get the chance, can you get the newspaper on the driveway?" What is the person asks, "When you come home, can you get the newspaper in the driveway?" Do you see the difference? "If" sounds like something is unattainable. It sounds as "if" it was not made for you. It seems like you don't really want something when you say if. The man tells his wife, "I will treat you better if you do what I say", but what he should really be saying is "When I communicate with you more effectively, you will be able to listen better; therefore, I will treat you better." The "when's and if's" can be in all kinds of scenarios.

What about when someone asks, "If I pass this test, can we go to the movies after?" Does this impact the way he takes his test? It definitely does. Think about it. He is not even sure that he will pass the test and uses the movies as his motivation, which is what he will think about during the test. How can he rephrase the question? "When I pass the test, can we go to the movies after?" Now, he has certainty about passing the test and will not even think about the movies until the test is over. He will do the best on his test because he wouldn't want to let his friend down, nor would he want to let himself down. His best interest will be in passing the test, and then pleasing his friend.

His priorities are in order. When he states, "When I pass the test", this is an affirmation to him that he will give it his all. He wouldn't be thinking about how his friend keeps thinking about the movies. Even his friend will pray with him, hope with him, and comfort him before and after the test. There is confusion for both himself and his friend about his preparation for the test when he begins to ask "If I pass the test…?" They will both question his ability. Before and after the test, there will be disunity between the man and his friend because the friend will think, "How can you take the test 'if' you are not ready?" instead of, "I trust you because every time you say you are ready, you always know 'when' to execute your plans." Using the word 'when' is more authoritative rather using the word 'if' in asking for a favor.

There is also uncertainty. They say, "If I get the chance, I will get that job" or "If I get enough money, I will buy a house". I think it is more important to believe in yourself and say the word "When" instead of "If." For example, "When I get the money, I am going to buy a Rolls-Royce." or "When I get to Virginia, I will get that job." The word "When" makes a bigger difference in your mind rather than the word "If", especially if you are referring to the future..

There are also thought-provoking and life enhancing questions. There are questions that can improve your performance. There are questions that will make you consider where you are located in society. I think questions are the most important ideations in our hearts and minds. You need to be asking yourself challenging questions in order to have a fulfilling life. Many people stop asking questions because they think they have found the answers they need, but they are only fooling themselves.

Here are 50 challenging questions that I believe will help you search your heart and mind:

1. Who am I and what do I want to represent?

2. What ways are you being perceived that you are unaware of?
3. Am I doing the things that I am specifically designed to do?
4. Why don't you do the things you know you should be doing?
5. What do you love the most about your work? Your family? Your friends? Your life? Your house? Your environment?
6. Is the decision you are making made by you or others?
7. Do you need to forgive anyone in your life right now or in your past?
8. How old would you be if you didn't know how old you are?
9. If I had to live with the decision I am about to make, would I be willing to?
10. How would the person I would like to be do the things I am about to do?
11. Do I live the life I most desire?
12. Do I have the right attitude about what I am doing right now?
13. Am I being myself?
14. Do I serve people the best way I can?
15. Do I surround myself with the best people I know?
16. Do I challenge myself the way I should?
17. What do I sort of values do I believe in?

18. Where am I going in my career path?
19. What can I do to be better?
20. Am I thinking the right thoughts right now?
21. Is this the life I really want to make myself happy?
22. Should I really be competing with who I am competing with?
23. How will I conquer the next task?
24. Am I doing the best thing right now at this very moment?
25. How can I make today my best day?
26. Do I feel good about myself?
27. How can I get more value out of life?
28. Do I need to speed up or slowdown in my style of living?
29. Do I have a good relationship with the people I surround myself with?
30. How can I make my relationships in my life better?
31. Where do you want to go in 5 years, 10 years?
32. What do you want to do in 5 years, 10 years?
33. Who am I becoming?
34. Do my values align with my work?
35. Are you too content with life?

36. Which is worse, failing or never trying?
37. Do I like where I are heading? If not, what can I do to change?
38. Who would you like to meet and how can you meet them?
39. What would you say if you met the person you always wanted to meet?
40. What are you most thankful for?
41. What is the change that I must make today?
42. If you have all of the money in the world, what would you do with it?
43. Do I need to act more urgently?
44. What is something I must do before my life is over?
45. Do I do meaningful work that helps others and add value to people and society?
46. What is the best use of my time?
47. How should I react to my present circumstances?
48. What can I do to plan better?
49. Do I make the right connections that will take me to where I need to go?
50. Do I live half-heartedly or whole-heartedly?

Hopefully, these questions have made you think thoroughly. There are millions of questions that you can ask yourself and others. Questions will help you navigate in this world. Never stop asking questions because there are infinite amounts of information that you need to know. As long as you ask the proper questions, your life will turn out far better than you could ever expect. Successful people ask better questions, and as a result, they get better answers. Shouldn't you be asking questions like the boss you are?

4

The Value of Time

"Time = Life, Therefore, waste your time and waste of your life, or master your time and master your life."- Alan Lakein

Different cultures value time in different ways. Some cultures do not consider time as valuable. They tend to live life as it comes. Other cultures treat time as if it were going to expire in twenty-four hours. I recognized the different ways in which people value time. China is a very relationship oriented country. Many locations within China that I have visited place less of an emphasis on time. It was the same when I visited Spain and a dozen other countries around the globe. There is a saying in Europe, "Americans measure time in decades, Europeans in centuries, and Asians in millenniums." All countries have developed in different ways and their culture determines much of their usage of time.

For instance, the Great Wall of China was built millenniums ago in 206 B.C. There are many cathedrals and bridges in Spain which were over 500 years old. But in America, since gaining our independence, we have made stupendous growth. In a little over 400 years since the expedition of Christopher Columbus, America has grown faster than any other country in the entire world. This made me think, "How have we grown so quickly in the past few centuries, and more recently in the past few decades, in regards to all of our technological advances?"

The reason is elementary. Our forefathers, business pioneers, philosophers, leaders, and teachers have dedicated their lives to their work by utilizing their time to work effectively. We have waited a long time to get what we have today and yet, we take most of it all for granted. Very often, we become complacent because we don't realize what they have established for us in this great nation of ours. Many times, we let minutes and hours go down the drain, barely thinking about how much time we really have. Some of us are far less productive than our predecessors. We waste our valuable time when there are so many things to choose from, but no clear distinction of what should really be the priority in our lives. What do we do with all of these opportunities?

Many of us lack the purpose that our predecessors had because we haven't realized what they have done for us. Many of us fail to create because we believe, in a way, that practically everything exists already. We feel that if we put our ideas to use, it will be shut down because someone has already thought of it in Australia, Egypt, or maybe even Zimbabwe. Since we cut ourselves short, we need to realize that there isn't really much competition, unless we make it for ourselves. You have so many opportunities to create something valuable, especially in the most complicated places. Your contribution is tremendous and thousands of people are waiting for you to deliver the results that they don't even know they want yet. Everyone is looking for a way to do something easier and faster.

In order to make a diligent study of time, we must realize that we will never master time, but we should never let time master us. Do you know how much time you have? Many people do not know how many hours are in the week, let alone a month or a year. Understanding time is the best way that you can break free and contribute your value to society. I will give you a quick way to measure.

There are a total of 168 hours in a week. Let's average our work week to 68 hours. This is more than enough for the average person to be working. This will also round our number to 100 hours. I will call these 100 hours discretionary hours. They are the number of free hours in which you will have in a week. Please remember that we took the 68 hours out of the week, which we will allocate for working purposes. This is how it breaks down: 168 hours-68 hours=100 hours.

Now we have 100 hours available after work, but we still need to sleep. We will now estimate that the average person will need 60 hours of sleep. This is more than enough for a professional or working-class person. It is said that you will perform on a high level at 7 to 8 hours. We are rounding numbers for this case. This will allow you over 8.5 hours to rest per day, which gives you plenty of time for rest.

Finally, we have 40 hours of discretionary time remaining. This means that we can do anything in the world that we want. Travel, read, take time with the family, and use our time leisurely.

We have more options than ever before and can choose up to millions of opportunities or distractions to pursue. Many of us choose the wrong things because we do not value the limited time God gave us on His planet. As I mentioned earlier, we do not appreciate all that we have and tend to take things for granted because they come so easily. If you wanted to be the best, you would follow your dreams and use your entire time to pursue your passion and purpose.

**Time Breakdown —
168 Hours Total = 68 Hours for Work + 60 Hours to Sleep + 40 Hours of Discretionary Time**

Let me share with you three systems of time that you can use to become the most productive in your life. These three systems of organizing time can alter the way you perform every day of your productive life. They can be used to measure the past, present, and future. One of the most powerful management tools is to know that "If time isn't measured, it isn't managed." You must measure your time and be able to manage it in order to be successful.

Here are three useful devices which measure and manage time:

1. **Keep a Journal**

   (Past)

2. **Having a To-Do list or Agenda**

(Present)

3. Setting Goals and Strategies

(Future)

1. Journal- Keeping a daily record of what you are doing allows you to process your progression. It allows you to keep track of your past. You can then review what you have written and learn from that time in which you have lived. I will give you a personal example of how I keep my journal. When I was sitting at a particular conference November 2nd, 2012, I saw the speaker give a fabulous presentation that I deeply admired. I prayed that, one day, I may be doing what he is doing. Can you believe in exactly one year I was giving a presentation? And guess who was sitting in my audience? It was the man who was presenting the year before. It was the same date that I had seen him just the year before--November 2nd, 2013! How did I know that it took exactly one year? Because I recorded it in my journal. Why did I record it? Why did it matter? Because I wanted to see the tremendous progression I would make. It was a great opportunity to look back on and I will be able to cherish it as long as I live. Without it being written down, I would have forgotten about it and it is likely that no one would be able to remind me of that event. Do you use a journal in this manner to record your life?

A journal can also be a good tool for reflection. When you look back and see how far you have come and what you have done, this allows you to reflect and see where you were in the past and how far you have come. Looking back allows you to review from your mistakes, see what you learned, and reminisce over the times you once had. With a journal, you can record jokes, stories, ideas, philosophies, events, people, and music that you prefer. You can keep track of quotes, books, and all sorts of information and facts all in a bound version.

In the past, I used to write things down on scraps of paper and toss it in my pockets, only to find that my disorganization led to the trash can. A journal captures the very essence of life and allows you to relive all of your experiences just as you had before in a meaningful way. It is the greatest tool with which to reflect and grow. Best of all, it is for you and your family to admire in the future. It is one of the best ways to remember how great your life is operating. Keeping a journal will also allow your grandchildren to know you better. They will read the stories about you and their imaginations will go wild after they hear about all of your secrets and fantasies. It's different when they hear about your vintage Volkswagen Beetle versus seeing pictures and reading stories about it. You will be a legend in your family.

In ancient times, people would pass down stories or write on the walls of the cave, but today Wal-Mart sells journals for about one dollar. Pens at the bank are free. Take 10-20 minutes every day to record your life. If you get anything out of this whole book, I want you to do this the most. It is one of the most valuable pieces of information in this book. Keep a journal and know who you are. Keeping an inventory of your past can help you better predict what you can do better in the future. In the long run, it is worth the dollar you invest.

"Always carry a notebook. And I mean always. The short-term memory only retains information for three minutes; unless it is committed to paper you can lose an idea for ever." — Will Self

2. To-Do Lists or Agendas- I found this to be of extraordinary help. Some people keep to-do lists only for meetings, grocery shopping, and packing for vacations, but they often forget to take into account their daily tasks of the day. Each day brings a surfeit of surprises and we need to make room for them. Do you try to do too much in a day? Perhaps you may be doing 15-20 tasks per day when you should really be focusing on the top 4-6 per day. Think about this: If you start were reading 15 different books at the same time, would you enjoy them all? If you gave 15 children individual attention, would they feel special love? What about if you listened to 15 different songs at once? If you gave 15 tasks all of your attention at the same time, will you have any focus? It is highly unlikely.

Your attention is diverted and is weakened because of you natural inability to manage these tasks all at once. We must focus on one task at a time. Everyone knows this, but few people do it. As we hear people say, "He is a jack of all trades, and a master of none." I do not think that this is a compliment most of the time. It usually means that a person has various skills and is mediocre at all, but proficient at none. Being a multi-tasker is not ideal either. You can't do two or three things at a time and be good at it. It is too unfortunate that 'multi-tasking' has become an acceptable theme. Most multi-taskers do activities, but seldom perform due to all the busy work that they are occupied with. A person should be able to master at least one thing in their lifespan. Aim for mastery and you will be successful.

This is how you do it. When you get off of your 9-6 job, do only the most important 2-4 tasks and no more. Focus on the most important and do the least important last. Most people are ineffective because they minimize their strengths trying to please everyone and everything. They take the shotgun approach, which has no aim. It is unlikely that you can work out, garden, read, plan, think, watch television, cook, take your kids out, eat, and walk the dog in five hours in the most effective way. You can probably do it, but you would be cheating the attention of some of the tasks. You won't be able to do all of them to the best of your ability. Cut that out. Do less, get more. Don't major on minors.

Try not to multi-task. Focus on what is really important. Keep a to-do list of 4-6 items per day and knock it out as you build a system of accomplishments that will stimulate your amygdala. As you go through the list, cross off everything that you have accomplished. This will give you more strength and enthusiasm because your mind will be programmed to know that you are producing. Eventually, you will find yourself taking on bigger tasks after you are able to master the smaller ones.

"Failing to plan is planning to fail." - Alan Lakein

I set my to-do list for ten minutes each night before I sleep and my subconscious mind takes it over and allows the plans come to fruition. Our subconscious mind works to find ways to achieve what we plan on accomplishing. Write down what you need to do right before you retire at night. Try to plan one day ahead. Make sure that every day you are always planning. If you focus on your plans, no one can come along and put you in theirs because you will be focused.

Follow the five P's: Proper Planning Prevents Poor Performance. Know what you want and know what you want to be able to reject as many opportunities will come each day. By planning for the next day, you will be able to seize the right opportunities faster and capitalize on your priorities. On the subsequent day, you will have brand new ideas cooking in your oven when you put the right ingredients right in front of you. You will be smooth like the old infomercial with Ron Pupiel: Just set it and forget it!

3. Goals and Strategies- A goal is the navigation system to get to our destination. Strategies are ways by which we set forth to reach our goals. You must have a strategy outlined so that you can pursue your goals. To set goals, we must first find the right vehicle and locate the right road to pursue. There are many vehicles and there are many roads. All you have to do is choose the right goals and strategies that work for your particular purpose. You must fervently believe that once you establish a plan with a definite purpose, there is nothing that will ever get in your way.

Imagine that you have an interview at your dream job. You planned everything out one week in advance. You found the perfect outfit to wear, you learned the right words to say, and you researched the company like you never researched before. Well, what will happen? Let's say you go to the interview in a taxi, but there is a car wreck ten minutes before you enter your destination. You know you can't wait in the taxi any longer, so you decide to get out and run to the destination because you have only ten minutes to get there before you are late. As you weave through the cars and zigzag through the people on the sidewalk, you begin to imagine how perfectly you will act during your interview. You run into the building and you expect everyone to help you find your interview room as you reach the office building for your interview.

Finally, you reach the office and you look at your watch, realizing that there are two extra minutes to spare. You take a deep breath and confidently walk in. You eventually relax and the heavy breathing and sweat that you eventually subsides. The interviewer asks you question after question as you ace them all in a spirit of absolute certainty. Your future employer gazes you into your eyes and realizes that you are the one as he begins to wrap up the harmonious interview. The interviewer tells you how stressed he was about finding the right candidate. In your mind you know you want to move up into the company to a specific position because of your goals and strategy. It is one of those interviews where you know you got the job. You gladly shake his hand and walk out fearlessly.

Did you achieve the goal? You definitely did. Could anyone stop you? Of course not! The goal was to get your dream job. The strategy was to find the best outfit, research the company thoroughly, and practice the words you will use in interview. Conversely, what if you didn't know what you wanted as a job and you weren't sure about yourself? What if you put no thought into your outfit and into your word choice? What if you had no strategy or no goal in mind? You would still be stuck in traffic and suffer in the agony of doubt. You would end up blaming everyone but yourself. Do you see the difference? Be the man with a plan! Be the woman who is unstoppable. No one can seize you from the opportunity that is rightfully yours. Take responsibility and attain your goals with the proper strategies in place. You are the boss of your success!

Here is another example: What if the captain fired up the engine of a ship and said that he wanted to cross the Atlantic Ocean leaving the East Coast. You ask him, "Where are you going?" To his rejoinder, "The other side!" Would you trust him? Absolutely not. He is not specific and doesn't seem to know where he is going. It appears that he has no goals or strategy. Most likely, he will end up derelict on a deserted island because of his lack of planning.

What if he proclaims that he wants to leave the New York Harbor with twenty crewmates and that his ship is well-stocked for the adventure? They have ten different strategies of getting to the same destination or goal, and he is well-planned to leave to reach London at 11:20 a.m. sharp on December 25th, which is five days away from the current day. Would you trust him? Definitely! He has a specific goal and a strategy to achieve it within a reasonable time frame. If he happened to run into chaos, he would know how to handle it effectively because he has multiple crewmates and strategies to reach his goal.

"You need to overcome the tug of people against you as you reach for high goals."
-George S. Patton

We cannot be trusted unless we trust ourselves. To trust ourselves, we need to plan diligently. I plan every day. Every morning, I break out a fresh piece of paper and write down how I plan to achieve my goals and what strategies and actions must be taken either today or in the future. This is separate from writing a to-do list or an agenda. Use specific targets and dates and create multiple strategies to fortify your goals. Your goals must be driven by a unstoppable desire to achieve them. Be flexible if your course veers off track. This is inevitable. No goal or strategy is good enough to work perfectly as planned without a few bumps in the road. The road to your dream is always meandering. You must create multiple modifications if the playbook requires it.

The more specific your goals and strategies, the more likely you are to get to your target. Remember that your goal is your navigation system to your destination. Put your imagination to use and create the proper strategies to achieve your goals and reach the desired destination. Just like the interviewee and the captain, when you are prepared, you will receive help to get to where you need to be. You must have faith. Saint Paul proclaims that "faith is the substance of things hoped for, the evidence of things unseen." You must continually feed your faith and believing that your dreams will materialize. You must believe in yourself just as strongly and cultivate a self-image that parallels your goals. When you believe in yourself, everyone will believe in you.

This strategy is how I was able to be on the stage one year after I believed it. Goals are the future that you want. In the Bible, Mark 9:23 states, "If thou canst believe, all things are possible to those that believeth." Can you believe it? Do you believe that you will attain your goals this year with the proper strategies? When you set goals and strategies to achieve them, you will. A dull pencil is better than a sharp mind. We retain what we write down. Write down your goals right now and review them daily. This is a 10-15 minute process each day. You can take up to one hour or more per day if you really want to achieve your goals faster. Write one-year, three-year, five-year, ten-year, twenty-year goals and strategies if you have that kind of vision. If you goals do not get your excited, create new ones. Don't pursue goals that do not benefit you. Go after the goals that will make you far better than you are today.

You will be more motivated than ever to achieve your goals. I teach goal-setting at my seminars all over the country. If this is something that you struggle with as I did, get it adjusted by paying a professional to help you set goals and create strategies. Learn how to do it the right way. I did, and the cost of the lesson was paid years ago. The doors will be opened; all you have to do is be willing to have the determination to walk through them. The goals are waiting for your arrival.

You must practice these time-management habits daily if you want to reap the reward. There are too many people working without the proper systems to manage where their time is going. That is why they never get anywhere. Most people end up running in circles because they do not know where they are headed. The minutes are long, but the years are short. Don't go to the grave unfulfilled. Take action now.

Remember, if you are failing to plan, you are planning to fail. Take advantage of your life by keeping track of your time. Abraham Lincoln once said that if he had 8 hours to chop down a tree, he would invest 6 hours to sharpen his ax. If he had to prepare, so should you! Get that dream job you always wanted. Go ahead and start to develop your own business. Do what you have always longed to do by keeping track of your time with these three measuring and management devices. It will pay off in the long haul and you will find that you saved plenty of time because of it. By using your time effectively, you can be among the best and brightest. Keep true to the 5 P's- Proper Planning Prevents Poor Performance. The United States of America and your fellow humans all over the world will love you even more because of your diligence with time.

You Are The Boss!

To recapitulate:

1. Journal- Past

2. To-Do List or Agenda- Present

3. Goals and Strategies- Future

"Time is what we want most, but
what we use worst." - William Penn

5

Five Levels of Listening

"All who have ears, let them hear!" - Jesus Christ

Listening is essential in your life. You must be able to listen to yourselves as well as listen to others. Listening helps us understand our present situation. You understand why certain things work the way they do by listening. You learn the most by listening to what people say. You can see your own thoughts as people speak to you. When you listen to them, you can ascertain what they are thinking in their minds and also what they may be thinking about you too.

You will find that the more you listen, the more people will appreciate you. God made two ears and one mouth for a reason and that reason is most likely so you can listen more than you speak. Listening can be a struggle at first, but once you understand how it works, it will become much easier. It takes great efforts to become a better listener because most people like to give advice, opinions, and facts. People are always excited about what they have learned recently. There are five levels of listening and we have all participated in each level. They are as follows:

1. **Ignoring-** This is when you are indifferent to the subject of discussion or the person who is discussing it. Ignoring is when you completely neglect everything that is being said because you are in your own head. Trillions of words are ignored because people often think that they have heard something before. We live in a 'know it all' society and everyone has access to information. We find it a waste of time to listen to others because we can easily find information in other resources. We will listen only when it's relevant or if our survival depends on it.

   People also ignore others because no one is really fresh with their verbiage. There tends to be too much stale language and typical methods of speaking are rampant. People often engender their trite and platitudinous deliveries to mundane subjects. They talk about superficial things like the weather, news, sports, and pop culture. It's comparable to eating the same ole' cheese pizza each week, no matter how much you love it, you get sick of it! We need new toppings! Many people are bored with what everyone is talking about. Mix your language up as best as you can. Put substance in your conversation and avoid ordinary tactics. Use ordinary conversation only if you are building rapport with another person.

We live in a melting pot society, rather than an assembly line. Instead of conforming to typical conversations, learn how to provoke thoughts with your salient words. It will bring the best out of the minds that are being allowed to consistently be dulled by non-usage and unstimulating conversations.

Some people often ignore because they do not believe that a person can edify them, therefore they repudiate the speaker. They do not see the credibility in what the person is saying because they are incongruent with their message. It is like having an obese man tell you what diet will work best for you. It could be that the person who is listening may be seeking health advice and a construction worker is telling them everything that they heard from Dr. Oz on television. It could even be that the person keeps rambling after you ask them a simple question.

Some people simply do not know when to ease off and stop speaking altogether. This can cause a listener to ignore completely and zone out into the next dimension. Perhaps, the listener hears a foreign language that they cannot comprehend or they may be xenophobic. It could be that they may not like you personally. When a person ignores, it will be difficult to gain credibility, but it is still possible once you understand the reason for their ignorance.

2. **Pretending-** People often dump information, emotions, stories, statistics, news, and all sort of garbage on us. It can

sometimes be inescapable to walk away from these trivial discussions because they may not know that you aren't interested. You may pretend to listen because you work with this person. You pretend to listen because you know that they are leaving in the next 30 minutes, so you nod your head as they tell you about their 4th grade son making the hockey team after they have been trying for several years of failed attempts. You may also pretend to listen because you like someone to know that you appreciate them, but your mind is occupied with other things. We have all been in this situation before.

You may also pretend to listen when you respect a particular person. You could have great respect for your teacher, but as soon as they start talking about politics, you know it is time to tune out respectfully as they ease into another tirade that you have heard before. Many pretend to listen to their spouse because they love them unconditionally, but they have heard enough of what they want to do in the future when the children leave home or when they retire. We often pretend to listen to the people that we live and work with because of the amount of time that we invest with them.

You can usually tell when a person is pretending to listen when they divert their eyes, change the subject, or respond tragically to your statements. You may be telling them how you ate oatmeal for dinner last night and they start to ask you about the steak dinner. People are usually hurt when they find out that someone that they are speaking to is pretending to listen to them. It is becoming more common in this world of distractions, so people are becoming less sensitive to those that ignore them.

The listener who is pretending to listen is often thinking about their thoughts and the next thing they can say to make themselves sound and/or feel good. They are formulating their responses as you realize that they only wished that you could stop talking or that they can abruptly cut you off and say what they have wanted to say. Pivot your attention between the person and your ideas so that you are able to give them more of yourself in a constructive manner. Don't think about the next idea you want to discuss until the other person has finished speaking.

You can gain credibility with the individual who is pretending to listen by catering to their needs instead of your own. Usually, they are tired of being talked to and just want to be heard for once. They want to be cared for. John Maxwell said it beautifully, "People don't care about what you know until they know how much you care." When people are pretending to listen, they look at you, but their minds are focused on their trip next month in Cancun, Mexico. When you see them day dreaming, try to find out what they are thinking about and cater to their conversation. You will win them over instantly when you start talking about Cancun, Mexico. By doing this, you will see that two minds unify and everyone will be happy.

3. **Selective-**The selective listener may often be thinking about ways in which they can benefit by the conversation, thus, allowing them to catch the key words and phrases to keep the conversation flowing. This person is genuinely searching for something more out of the conversation, but may not always ask directly. They will usually suggest it to you by the way their body reacts to what you are saying to them.

   Selective listening can be changed by a shift in body language and deeper eye contact. Sometimes you can just simply mirror their behaviors. Usually, the selective listener can be confronted with facial expressions, vocal variety, unique digressions, and other elements of surprise. I once took a selective listener to a deeper level by simply changing the scenery by walking towards a different direction. We went from a rambunctious dinner party that was overcrowded to a serene fountain in the courtyard with scattered individuals. Our conversation changed instantly because of the dynamic and tranquil atmosphere.

   Sometimes you can catch a good conversation in a bad spot. By simply moving your location, you can indubitably penetrate their cranium with your intellectual storytelling. You could even tap your shoes or make an outlandish gesture to get their full attention. You can always get a selective listener to pay attention to you when you figure out why they are listening to you in the first place.

   Being around a selective listener can be even more dangerous than the listener who ignores or pretends. Let's say that you are talking to a selective listener and they heard what they wanted to hear. Maybe they caught a key word or euphemism and they get stuck on that point. They will most likely ignore everything you say after that because they are dwelling on what you previously said. Sometimes you can turn a selective listener completely off by saying something that offends them, even if you didn't know it. They won't even tell you, but that's just the way human nature works. Another thing that can happen is that you say something that amazes them, but they get stuck on that one idea and stop listening to you for the rest of the way. Perhaps, you will want to pause or ask them a question to get them back to your conversation.

It could even be worse than that. What about if you are talking to a person who loves to gossip to other people? The world is full of these people. They will selectively listen to what you say and pick and choose what they want. They seek out specific bits of information and deceptively interrogate you until they get the answer that they were looking for. When they get the answer they want, they will take it to other people and manipulate the story. By the time you hear it again from someone else, it will be a different story and most likely something completely different than what you actually said. This happens every day. They are difficult to detect, but you will learn who they are because of the questions that they ask you and the responses that they give you what you get into dialogue with them. Beware of this indirect attack. You don't want your words to get mixed up in the minds of others, especially if it is in your control. Watch what you say and to whom you say it to.

Overall, the selective listener can come in various forms. It is difficult to know who is selectively listening. The best way to know is to learn how you selectively listen. If you find yourself selectively listening, ask yourself, "Why am I selectively listening to this person?" Usually, you will find the answer and begin to change the way you approach others by the answer that you found.

4. **Attentive-** This listener tries to "read between the lines," attempting to discern the real meaning of the subject espoused by the other person. They are cognizant of who they are dealing with. They know who they are and where they are as well. This person is usually of the intellectual nature, but doesn't quite go into discourse with as much emotions as they should. These listeners sometimes put up barriers as protection to keep others from harming them. They listen very well, but they tend to not accept everything that is said, even if facts are being told. You can find this kind of skeptical listening by those who fold their arms or stare blankly at what you are saying.

   Usually when a person is listening on an attentive level, they may like what you have to say, but they are not speaking on the same terms. This tends to happen when people of different fields are working together; Their language is completely different. Here is a quick example of this: The sales and marketing department of a particular company thinks in terms of deadlines, quotas, and profit. They tell you about what people will see on the outside. The engineers of the company are focused on quality and durability, so they are talking about the intricacies that the sales and marketing department has no time to hear about. Even though they conflict intellectually because they are unable to compassionately understand the big picture and see why things in different areas work the way they do.

Sometimes attentive listening is similar to listening without understanding. Each person looks at each other and tries to understand what another person is saying, but the words do not make sense at all, no matter how intently they listen. This also happens with the use of jargon. When someone hears the computer man talk about 'interfacing' and 'clouding,' he cannot relate because he doesn't understand what those particular words mean. He then is too ashamed to ask because the computer man thinks he understood and continued the conversation in more jargon. He keeps asking himself, "What is interfacing and clouding have to do with me?" even while the computer man keeps rambling. Sometimes in this case, it is not important to know what certain words mean, but if it is important, you better find out what the words mean and comprehend them fully before major mistakes are made.

This is what happened to the Space Shuttle Challenger in 1986. Around 8:30 a.m. on Tuesday, January 28, 1986 in Florida, the seven-member crew of the Space Shuttle Challenger was strapped into their seats. Though they were ready to go, NASA officials were busy deciding whether it was safe enough to launch that day. It had been extremely cold the night before, causing icicles to form under the launch pad. By morning, temperatures were 32° F. If the shuttle launched that day, it would the coldest day of any shuttle launch.

Safety was a major concern, but NASA officials were also under pressure to get the shuttle into orbit quickly. Climate and technical malfunctions had already caused previous postponements from the original launch date, which was January 22nd. If the shuttle didn't launch by February 1, some of the science experiments and business arrangements regarding the satellite would be jeopardized. Plus, millions of people, especially students across the U.S., were waiting and watching for this particular mission to launch. The pressuring deadlines from everyone and the miscommunication made it one of the worse NASA disasters that ever happened. Attentive listening is the epitome of listening without full understanding.

People sometimes learn on the attentive level of listening and many words are retained. Sometimes, the person who pays attention to the speaker won't remember who told them something special that they have learned, but they will remember the lesson or story they taught them. Usually, the intellectual level can stimulate a person, but there can still be something done on the emotional level. This will take us into the fifth level of listening.

5. **Empathetic-**This listener's heart and soul goes into what is to be understood. You are giving it everything you have on this level. This person is compassionately listening and looking forward to everything the other person is saying. You are providing all of your attention as a listener, and that is exactly what the speaker needs for them to give you their best words.

    My favorite business philosopher and speaker, Jim Rohn once proclaimed, "Attention is the greatest gift you can give anybody." When you get deep with a person, you will find that you will be able to connect with them on rare and even spiritual levels. The empathetic listener discerns what the conversation is really about because of its distinctive harmony.

    Pour your heart out and feel the words and see the pictures in your mind. This type of listening is the most stimulating and can leave you mesmerized for days. It can even impact the way you think every day and ultimately be life-changing. You will feel an emotional connection with the person you are engaged with. You can even touch, rub, hug, or kiss someone when you listen on the empathetic level because it exhibits true love in the conversation. Empathetic listening makes you want to bring the person home or become their best friends. Sometimes you will naturally exchange a phone number or business card because you have connected with the stranger so deeply that you feel as if you need to remain in touch with them.

Credibility is established on this level. It doesn't matter who the person is, where they come from, or even their appearance, you truly feel the love for this person. You completely trust the person on this level because they have connected emotionally with you. It is common to listen with your eyes, because your ears won't suffice, although you'll still get an ear-gasm on this level of listening. No one will be offended when you listen on the empathetic level.

It is the best way that you can render love to someone. You rarely get the chance to meet someone who will listen on the empathetic level, and when you do, make sure you take full advantage of it. You have experienced this level of listening before and you know that it is worth the effort. Go ahead and try listening on the empathetic level. It will change your life and those you speak and listen to. You are the boss!

"Wisdom is the reward you get for a lifetime of listening when you'd have preferred to talk."- Doug Larson

6

How to ACT like a Leader

"Open your eyes, look within. Are you satisfied with the life you're living?" -Bob Marley

I have been studying leadership for quite some time now and have come to realize that leadership means different things to different people. What leadership means to you isn't what leadership means to me, and what leadership means to me isn't what leadership means to you. We all have different definitions of what leadership really means and I wanted to find out the real answer. I went to the dictionary to look up the word 'leadership,' and this is what I found: the position or function of a leader, a person who guides or directs a group, or the tendency of being a leader. None of these clearly defines leadership, and I needed to find the real answer. I started looking across the east coast of the United States of America. I called interviewed hundreds of professional people everywhere I went, but only found circuitous and superficial answers. I even traveled the world to find the real answer to what leadership could mean.

From my observation of human beings, I found that leadership can be defined in just four words: "People See, People Do." It can be likened to the philosophy of "monkey see, monkey do." I am sure you have heard of this before. Let's explore an example of this. What if two monkeys are together and one decides and says to the other, "I want three bananas." He starts to climb the tree and the other monkey watches to see if he can do it. The monkey who is watching the other monkey climb says to himself, "I can do that too!" and he believes in his leader and cherishes him. He may even start to believe in his own abilities as he watches his leader perform. His leader gives him a boost of confidence that he did not have before.

Human beings are the same way. When you see a commendable person do something you admire, you admit to yourself, and sometimes to the other people, that they are your leader(s). This means that leadership is a choice. You can choose your leaders and you can choose to be a leader as you emulate leaders who have helped you. Technically, by this definition, we are all leaders because other people will study and learn from us. Realize that people are watching your behavior, which means that all of us have the capacity for leadership. When you think of it, you have to realize that people are always watching each other. They are watching what you say, they are watching how you dress as well as your overall appearance, and most of all, and they are watching the way you ACT.

Now I want you to learn how to ACT like the leader that you are. I am not talking about Broadway shows, commercials, or the movies. I am talking about the three step process in which you can utilize to become a better person. Knowing how to ACT like a leader is an acrostic that spells out three words: audacious, contagious, and tenacious. I truly believe that you learn how to ACT like a leader in an effectual way because of this method. First, I will tell you what this means, and then I will give you examples in which you can use to utilize the method I have expounded.

Become audacious. Some people think of being audacious as being bodacious bold and brassy, overtly ostentatious, or ruthlessly reckless, but that's not what I intend to deliver to your mind. To satisfy your curiosity, I would like to think of it as being impeccably inventive, officially original, and completely courageous. This is the kind of person who is never afraid to take risks. By the way, if you didn't know, risk is the new safe. You cannot get out of life alive. You can either be on the field playing the game, or you can be in the masses in the stands watching the game with several thousand others who speculate. Yes, life is a game. The safest thing to do in life is to take a risk. Be sure to switch it up.

Try a new restaurant, drive a different kind of car, do something you have never done before. It might catch on. You have to reach beyond your comfort zone. If you don't know what your comfort zone is, that means that you are probably in it. You cannot be growing if you are in your comfort zone. You will not be comfortable if you are growing. You must be willing to stretch out and see the possibilities presented to you. Take action upon them once you realize that what you are doing is right. In order to be audacious, you must have a passionate desire to continue on the quest that lies before you. You will be an influential force upon those who you come in contact with and they will be readily able to assist you in reaching your goals.

Go where you are afraid to go and do what you are afraid to do. Be who you are afraid to be. Success can be the biggest fear to most people. The majority of people are unwilling to it deprives them of the success that could be taking place in their lives. If 95% of the people in your area are going one way, be audacious and take the initiative to go the opposite direction. You will find that unexpected resources in unexpected places at unexpected times will show up by unexpected people. When you are audacious, the unexpected will happen and everyone will grow from your ability to be yourself in your truest form. Go ahead and do something that you have never done before. You are the Boss!

Next, **be contagious.** This is when it catches on. When you start by doing something audacious, it automatically becomes contagious. This is when you have the 'Spirit of Magnetism.' Because it is inventive, original, and courageous on your behalf, it appears that not only you like it, but other people do as well. After you find something that works, you will begin to see other people to imitate you. You draw people in because of who you are, what you've done, and where you are going. People will respond positively to you when you seem to know where you are going. They will applaud you, adore you, and affirm you in almost everything that you do. You will be acknowledged in the highest places in society.

However, beware; you don't want to spook them out by showing them that you know what they are doing. This may cause them to lose face and stop doing whatever they were emulating from you. Just let them enjoy themselves. If they acknowledge that you have lead them to be the way they are currently acting, just appreciate the moment and go be contagious somewhere else, because there will always be someone that needs your help.

Being contagious requires you to have a lot of personal power and responsibility. People will question you and challenge your beliefs because they are different from theirs and the masses of people who think 'normally.' They will begin to test you and see if you really believe in what you are doing. This may be in a direct form or indirect form. A direct challenge will be a question or statement directed to what you are doing. An indirect challenge will be subtle, yet still detectable. If not detected and confronted, either attack can be deleterious. Whether someone challenges you directly or indirectly, you will be able to respond accordingly. They will not defeat you because you are the one who has the influence over them due to your ability to ACT. Realize that when you are contagious, it can be a highly enviable position because of your ability to command the attention that is unattainable to them.

Finally, **be tenacious.** Be passionate, have faith, keep persisting. When you are tenacious, you are doing more than you are paid to do. You will start to volunteer and not think of how you will be repaid. You know that it will come back in some way or another. You will also begin to go the extra mile. You will make personal sacrifices for others in order to make everything work out, no matter what the cost is. A tenacious person never gives up, even if persecution and terror is at its pinnacle.

There are several options once you've acknowledged that you have influenced people. Being tenacious enforces that you are an authority on whatever subject you have conquered, and now you have to be unyielding to your method that is fascinating everyone. You are now audacious because you are trying something new, contagious because you have a lot of fans, but now what? You can be tenacious. You have options now. You can choose to keep doing what you are doing, or you can try something else. It is usually where you breakthrough in life and desire to keep going in the direction you are currently heading or deviate into another direction in a controlled manner.

You can even go back to what you originally did prior to deciding to become audacious. However, I typically find that going back to what you did before you were audacious is very difficult to do. Be so tenacious that no one can corrupt your unshakable manner. Never let anyone outdo you, especially on that which you have started. Being tenacious allows you to work on your craft at a rate in which it would be impossible to fail. As stated before, it requires you to do more than what you are paid to do. It requires you to go the extra mile. Being tenacious will bring the best out of you in every circumstance.

Here are some clear-cut examples:

Have you ever been shopping and see something that you know you need to buy, even if you have never tried it before? One time, I went to the mall and suddenly I was entranced by the sight of a fedora. Although I have not worn one before, it was one of those dazzling hats that I knew I had to buy. I had to be audacious, so I tried it on, got a couple free opinions from the department store clerks, and then left. I knew I would be elegantly caparisoned when I bought it. I then began to wear it often at school because people loved it on me. I got complements daily, and that was the affirmation that it was right.

I became the guy with the hat, and I was contagious. Everyone on the college campus knew who I was because of this hat and suddenly, not to my surprise, I saw someone else wearing it. I confronted him with positive acknowledgement and he was astonished at my approval. As the months passed by, and I saw numerous variations of fedoras on campus. They all consisted of different styles and colors. Most individuals wearing the hats never knew that I started the trend. Everywhere I went, people were praising me. Of course, like anyone, being contagious made me confident. People did affirm, adore, and applaud me. And yes, I was acknowledged. Everyone loves to be acknowledged.

This made me imagine better hats, and I became tenacious. I bought dozens of fedoras and wore different ones every day. Eventually, I found one to match every outfit that I own. I haven't stopped wearing them since my very first encounter. I believed that there would be a hat for each outfit that I had. I searched diligently to find the right ones. In due time, I was able to get the best hats for myself. Now that's how you ACT!

How can this apply to you?

Easy! Set a trend by doing something that has never been done before. Move the coffee pot and watch people either praise you or dispute your reasoning, depending on how audacious you are about it. It's possible that they'll accept it and start to move things in the office, like the trash can or their family photos, making your efforts contagious. They'll think, if he or she can move the coffee pot, I can move my calendar. Promptly, you'll zoom off to your next project and become tenacious by changing the light bulbs, or throwing the first pizza party on Monday. After all, you know how to ACT because you are the boss!

Inevitably, when you do ACT like the person you are, it will cause reactions. Naturally, not all people like surprises, and when you catch them off guard, they may become defensive. Some people will support you and will enjoy the surprise when you ACT in the right way. Learning how to ACT like the leader you are may be risky at first and it is best to know that the rewards are higher than not being able to ACT like the leader you are. When you begin to ACT like the person you are, you will hold a commendable position, whether it is in the community, at church, at work, at the gym, in your family, or anywhere else you would go. Life is about becoming yourself.

To Reiterate:

Be Audacious-Be spontaneous, original, and bold. Take a risk and try something that you have never done before. Go outside of your comfort zone and do what you have always been afraid to do.

Be Contagious-Your actions and personality will be memorable. Possess the 'Spirit of Magnetism' by attracting others because of your behavior. Gain confidence by building on what you have created.

Be Tenacious-Don't just stop, keep going. Repetition and practice is required. Be sure to do more than you get paid to do. Go the extra mile. Keep working on it. Possess the kind of perseverance whereby you become unstoppable because of your faith.

Now go out there and ACT like the person

you are because You are the Boss!

7

Becoming a Better Communicator

"The single biggest problem in communication is the illusion that it has taken place".
-George Bernard Shaw

Do you want to become a better communicator? Perhaps you want to speak all over the country, give presentations at work more smoothly, or improve your interpersonal skills. If you would like to communicate more effectively, there are many things you can do. I improved my speaking skills substantially by joining Toastmasters. Surprisingly, not many people know about this organization with over 300,000 people. Toastmasters was instrumental in the transformation of my life in regards to communication, leadership, and business skills.

You can join Toastmasters by going to Toastmasters.org and searching by city or zip code. When you join Toastmasters, stay consistently involved in the meetings. Give as many speeches as you can. Sign up for different roles and learn about what you can do to improve your communication skills. Speaking among a group of people is all about confidence and you should be comfortable about what you plan to say as you step in front of a group of people. Even if you are talking intimately among your loved ones, what you say, how you say it and when you say it is crucial.

Without the ability to communicate effectively, you will often find that you are at a severe disadvantage. You won't be able to effectively seek promotion, whether it is in work, church, and even life in general. It is imperative that you immerse yourself to become a better communicator. Nothing is better than someone giving the right words at the right time. It sends tingles up your spine and penetrates the cranium. Proper communication will increase the joy between the correspondents and there will always be satisfaction. Most importantly, you feel better in your heart because of the kindness and words someone used to comfort you.

The following are six habits on which you can use to communicate more effectively. These habits have been valuable to me in regards to communication. They have promoted me on the highest levels of achievement. These habits can help you immensely in all areas of your life.

They are the following:

1. Read the **Dictionary (or Thesaurus)**. There are two kinds of people in the world: There are the few who look up words in the dictionary, and the overwhelming mass of people who decide that it is not worth the effort. My first suggestion to you so that you may become a better communicator is to read the dictionary. Focus on learning the words that you will use in your daily conversations and

writing. For every word you look up, you learn ten other words in the process through location and relation

Let me share a story about Malcolm X. I appreciated his diligence when he was found in a prison cell with a man named Bimbi. This man named Bimbi would dominate all of the conversations because of the knowledge that he had amassed over time. This made Malcolm envious. He knew that he could do better than he currently was doing at the time. He soon began to read; He could not understand the words, so he requested blank papers, pens, and a dictionary.

Malcolm began to list certain words, their pronunciations, and all of the ways that he could use the words he had found. Malcolm X became a great orator and spoke during the civil rights era with Dr. Martin Luther King Jr. It was because he took up a serious study upon becoming more knowledgeable in regards to the words he was using, thus, making him a phenomenal speaker. Many great orators, including myself, study the dictionary (and thesaurus) on a daily basis. It separates the average from the best.

You should be sure of the words you are using before you use them. Know the word's definition. For instance, when a person says that they will peruse a book, they sometimes think it means that they will skim over it. However, this means the exact opposite. If you peruse something, you are thoroughly reading it. Often times, we hear people using redundancies. These are sure to make you laugh once you think about what was truly said.

Here are some redundant and jargon words that I have heard in the past: Calculated risk, cautiously optimistic, credibility gap, communication gap, quantum leap, phase out, cutting edge, meaningful dialogue, peer group, considered judgment, learning experience. Just to name a few of the hundreds that exists. I could say more, but that would be excessively abundant (get it?).

"A man's character may be learned from the adjectives which he habitually uses in conversation." -Mark Twain

Often times, we give excuses for not having enough time to learn our language. We must realize that language is the one of two criterions that people tend to judge you on first. You could be the best-looking person, but as soon as you speak, people will know how to interact with you. Hence, you must develop a fascination and a command for the language that you use. Using the dictionary can help you enormously when you are beginning to build your vocabulary. I encourage you to read vocabulary building books. My favorite is from Johnson O'Connor. The title of his book is called "Johnson O'Connor Vocabulary Builder (1926)." I believe that it will change your life once you complete this excellent book. Words shape your world when you use them in the right way. You have plenty of word power and be crowned a potentate because you are the boss!

2. The best way to become more articulate in conversations is to practice your **pronunciations** until you have mastered the words in your immediate vocabulary. Many people say pro-noun-see-ay-shun, when it is pronounced pro-nun-see-ay-shun. Others say in-her-ant when the word is in-heer-ant. Often, this leads to their definitions of

the word(s) being wrong because they have confused words for the simple fact that they have mispronounced it. Another example some might say that word's origin is entomology; when they mean to say etymology. Entomology is the study of insects while etymology is the derivation of words. Just remember that there are no "N" in the word etymology!

Practice articulating words out loud as you study the dictionary and saying the words out loud. Enunciating words correctly will give you tremendous credibility and you will be able to think more clearly as you comfortably ease your words out. I remember certain words that I couldn't have said before that I have now mastered. Here are a few words I used to butcher: antithesis, promulgate, existentialism, and corroborate. Those may be easy words for you, but it took me a while to become familiar with them. There may be a few words that you know, but often avoid, because you have not acquainted yourself with them as best as you could of. An easy way to practice your pronunciations would be when you are driving in a car or reading a book. Keep saying words out loud as you commute to your location.

Try articulating challenging names too. There is nothing more impressive than correctly saying a foreign name. I knew a man who once broke down crying after someone pronounced his whole Russian name correctly. He said that no one said his full name since he came to America up until that time eight years ago. Do not avoid challenging words and names. Take them on, because they do exist. To work on pronouncing names, there are various peculiar names in the Old Testament. I bet you when you try to pronounce those names, all of your words will be crisper. If you can pronounce those names, you can pronounce any name.

Here is one last thought to ponder about words: Have you ever met a man that you found to be unusually spectacular? Perhaps there was something different about him in his presence or talent. Didn't you want to know his name? How about where he came from? What about what he does for work? It is the same for words. As we inquire about people and things, we must also know everything about the words we choose to use. Words are the tools by which we mold our minds. Read this paragraph again.

3. Another way to become a better communicator is by using the proper **body language (your gestures and posture)**. Some people gesture too much, some gesture too little. Gestures should add to what you are saying, not subtract. When you go to a city and talk to people, you find people that gesture all over the place. When someone who is reading a PowerPoint verbatim, they are less likely to gesture because they do not already know what they are going to say. They have to read and speak simultaneously.

By using gestures, you are able to convey your message in ways that you cannot verbally. Most of your communication derives from the gestures and expressions that you make. People are watching them and some will even tune your words out entirely, but they will pay attention to your gestures. Your gestures will give you power and flavor in your communication. Without strong gestures, you are an ordinary two-dimensional communicator.

Gesturing helps us to deliver the message in a more picturesque form. It can also help you get to the point much faster. Sometimes, I find that people get so caught up in gestures, that they forget their purpose of speaking, and so does the audience. Never confuse people with your gestures. Just do what works for you. Keep your gestures robust and congruent with your overall communication. You can also work on your gestures and facial expressions in the mirror once or twice per week for ten minutes. Facing yourself and your reactions are difficult at first, but you can learn a lot about yourself this way.

"As I grow older, I pay less attention to what men say. I just watch what they do."-Andrew Carnegie

Posture is an important attribute in regard to verbal and non-verbal communication. Your body language tells people who you are. People know a bum when they see one. They also know a strong and confident person by the way they speak and carry themselves. Using the right kind of posture will ensure people that what you are saying comes from the heart and show them your conviction. I see many people leaning on object when they talk. It shows they are unsure of themselves, unless they are tired. Sadly, I have also seen people slouching, crossing their arms and legs, and position their feet in funny ways when they are communication. It is always best to stand up straight while speaking with people.

Let me share a secret with you about body language. Sometime in the near future, take note of peoples' feet the next time you talk with them. Notice the direction they are pointing their feet. Peoples' feet will tell you their priority. If you are talking to someone and their feet are pointing towards the door, you better wrap up before you inconvenience them. Their feet are usually the most honest part of their bodies. It will tell you much about their feelings that most ways won't reveal.

You can tell who a person is by their posture some of the times. You can get a feel for a person's sense of character and dignity from their posture. It's easy to decipher if they are the type of person who you would prefer to work with. In order to communicate effectively, with the best posture, keep your arms and feet adjacent while standing. This will help you convey strength to your message. Try to be as symmetrical as you can be when you are standing. When you are sitting down and communicating, make sure that your hands can be seen. Open hands are usually more convincing and trustworthy than closed hands. Do not to slouch or put your elbows on any tables. Never allow the bottom of your feet to show. It can be perceived as being highly disrespectful to many cultures.

4. **Vocal Variety**-Using vocal variety will keep people interested. For instance, when you pick up the phone, use a high or low-pitch voice to answer. Try it now. Say "Hello!" in various tones. You can even try to sing your words for a dramatic effect. When you know how to use the most interesting instrument in the world, you can affect people in tremendous ways. A good way to clear your throat is to have a more appealing voice to exhale. When you try this, it will most likely work for you.

When people clear their throats it creates a cacophonous and could subtract from what you say, especially if you have a hoarse voice. Also, try not to cough and sneeze while communicating verbally. The best way to prevent sneezing is to stick your tongue to the roof of your mouth as soon as you feel a sneeze coming. The sooner you do this, the more effective it will be. If you have the hiccups, there are many remedies. I usually hold my breath until they are gone and it always works. There is nothing worse than sneezing, coughing, wheezing, hiccupping, and clearing your throat when you are trying to say something to someone, especially if you are before an audience of any kind. If you create habits on how to more effectively control your voice, these obstacles will be expunged in your verbal communication.

Vocal variety can quickly grasp the attention of someone while they are not listening. It could even promote laughter if done in the right way. It will enhance your ability to communicate and allow more color in conversations. It might send tingles up your spine when someone speaks in a voice that is variable. Try to play with your voice as much as you can. To be the best story teller, change your vocals to access different kinds of voices. This will add an impeccable spontaneity to your message. Vocal variety will take you far in verbal communication. It is one of the biggest secrets to mastering a successful conversation.

5. **Eye Contact** is important as well. I am amazed at how many people I find who cannot hold eye contact. There are some who cannot even look into the eyes of the person they are speaking to. The best prescription for this atrocity is to stare in the mirror for at

least five minutes per day. You can even use the mirror at traffic light stops while you are in your car. You will be amazed of how penetrating your eye contact will be. Another way is just to practice looking at people as you speak to them. Your eye contact will strengthen phenomenally.

Try to go for a little longer if you believe that it is possible to do so. When speaking to a small group of 10-20 people, look a different person in the eyes as you pause for a moment during your talk. Allow your eyes to work the room. Many rookie speakers will ignore a major section of the audience that they are speaking to because of the favorable expressions of the few. If you look at more people in the eyes, you will win them over, even if they are adamant to your message.

Another great and easy way to communicate is to smile. The best smiling is done with your eyes. Again, many people do not smile, but it will increase your ability to influence and communicate effectively. Smiling is an easy way to gain trust and in turn, improve your eye contact with other people. Make sure your smile is genuine. You need to be happy and filled with joy in order for this to happen. Smiling increases your face value. Your face value can also be increased by your eye contact with whomever you are speaking with at the moment.

If you are speaking to hundreds or thousands at a time, be sure to glance at sections in the crowd. They will know that you acknowledge them and may even think that you are looking at them as an individual. Be fair in eye contact with your superiors, as well as your inferiors. Never use eye contact to threaten, expose, or belittle people. Instead, use eye contact to encourage and love the people who you are trying to communicate with. Eye language is a contact sport, and the better you become at it, the more attention you will get and be able to give. Everyone loves attention!

6. Practice- This is one of the most neglected, but obvious things to do as a speaker and communicator (or any other profession involving repetition as a means to increase competence). In order to get better at anything, repetition is necessary. Practice takes time, but the time invested is well worth it. When you become the best communicator or speaker in a particular organization, it gives you the motivation to move into the next endeavor. When you know how to explain yourself and convey your ideas, you will be promoted on all levels of life.

It begins with practice. Before I give a speech of any kind, I make sure that I write out all of the details, practice at least twenty times, and record three of them. I then study each of them and practice in the mirror. I keep count on paper by using a tally system for each time I practice. I used to try to practice my speeches in a set amount of time, but I found that the amount of times I practice them is more important than the time in which I practiced. Find your own methodology and stick to your practice regimen. If you believe you should give one speech per month, schedule twelve as your goal for the year. If you want to be a professional speaker, schedule two-hundred speeches in a year after you quit your job and hire a coach. Make sure you stick to the plan.

The key to practicing is to set up the time in which you choose to practice your speeches. If you choose to practice that which is not a speech, for instance, a sales presentation or a panel discussion, try to make it as real as you can. Get all of your thoughts on paper as soon as you can. Remember, a dull pencil is better than a sharp mind. Practice writing out your methods of communication, whether it is a joke, a story, or an idea. You must practice until you are able to naturally bring parts of it into your daily conversation. Also, practice your presentation until people recognize that it is not staged and robotic. Your speeches should be authentic and have spontaneity.

Besides setting goals and practicing, the best way to prepare mentally is by closing your eyes and letting your imagination take you to the place that you are going to give the presentation. You will not be as surprised by the time that you get there and you will allow yourself to deliver the presentation in the most fascinating way, because you prepared by practicing. This form of visualization will help you to prepare in the greatest way possible. Preparation and practice will not make perfect, but it will set you up for eventual success.

I hope that by reading this chapter you have learned better ways to communicate. If you really want to become better at speaking and communication, watch great orators, speakers, leaders, and teachers. You can find many on internet and television talk shows, TED talks, radio, and seminars. Go to church and hear a good preacher. Some of my favorite speakers are Billy Graham, Jim Rohn, Earl Nightingale, Les Brown, Joel Osteen, Martin Luther King Jr., and TD Jakes. These are only a few. There are thousands of living examples today to choose from. Be sure to study humor also. Read many books and tighten up your use of words and phrases. Also, speak at an understandable pace and accentuate the words and phrases that are necessary. Also, repeat certain words and phrases that drive the point into the mind of the listener. Use a mixture of all of these to become a better speaker. The best way to learn is to just speak! You will soon become cogent in your communication skills. Communication is one of the best ways to refine your authority. Remember, you are the boss!

8

A.I.D.A

"Show people what they want and they will move Heaven and Earth to get it." - Frank Bettger

People have argued for centuries and have gotten into wars due to the growing demand for increasing their territories and possessions. In ancient times, people would enter villages and cities, which they would burn down, plunder destroy, cheat, and kill to ruthlessly obtain what was not theirs. This caused a lot of unnecessary bloodshed and the animalistic behavior which needed to be eradicated. One day, some wise soul asked himself "Wouldn't it be a wonderful idea to share my wheat to obtain that other man's gold?" This one idea set into motion the groundwork known as the bartering system.

He knew that if he offered something of value to the other person that they would consider some type of fair trade. This transaction was not easy because it had never been done before. It involved a lot of risk and persuasion. It required faith that one would not lose his life due to the uncertainty of the transaction. For instance, if a person entered a town with their goods, they could be robbed and killed for trusting the wrong persons.

Eventually, money came into play as the bartering system became more complicated. Money (paper and coins) was and still is the medium of exchange that would change the world. People strove to be more diplomatic and tactful as they continued to handle their affairs. No one wanted to fight violently anymore because there was something of value that they could have amassed they acted accordingly. This was especially true if they wanted to become a merchant, tradesman, farmer, skilled worker, or anyone who enhanced the value of the marketplace. Suddenly, people started to sell silk, porcelain, paper, drugs, massages, and everything under the sun in order to gain a profit.

Today, the most common things like water and air can be sold at premium prices. Everything in your house was either given or sold to you. They all exist because both parties wanted to gain in a transaction. We have a higher quality of life because of civilized trade. Nothing in this world moves without being sold. If you don't learn persuasion, you will be persuaded and tricked into all kinds of traps by manipulators in the marketplace. You will put you money where it should not go because you didn't understand the psychology of your own reasoning and it will cause you great frustration. It is best to understand the basics of persuasion, because you encounter it every day with hundreds, sometimes thousands of marketing messages.

"So long as new ideas are created, sales will continue to reach new highs." – Dorthea Brand

Everyone is in sales. You may or may not realize it but every day you are selling your products, services, and/or ideas. In this world of persuasion, you better understand how it works. Every day we are bombarded with mass media as they deliberately market everything they "think" you need. Hence, this is big reason why people get mad and often frustrated at those who are in sales. They think the car dealer is out to get them, the knives being sold won't work, or the service you render will only provide transient benefits. Unfortunately, we do live in a world of legerdemains and swindlers, but you must not let this stop you from gaining a perspective that will alter your state of thinking in regard to sales. Most people in sales are honest, only few are frauds.

I say all of that to say this. The system that I would like to introduce to you may solve some of the queries you formally had about marketing schemes. The system of which I refer to is called **A.I.D.A.**: *Attention, Interest, Decision, and Action.* This is a serious promotional technique that is used with big scale companies to market a variety of products and services to millions of people. First, I will give you one humorous example of this and then I will present you with the one of the most powerful methods that mass media uses this strategy to market goods and services.

Let us take the example of the home life. I will use myself for the first example. One Saturday I am sitting on my couch in my house. I got lonely after my wife left the house and was gone for four hours. I realize that I am bored and I need more entertainment than reading. During that time, I am waiting as I stare at the pages of my book and evade the responsibility of reading. Suddenly, she walks in the house. She is wearing the most impeccable outfit that I have ever seen. She gains my **attention**.

She begins to sing my favorite song, "Strangers in the Night" by Frank Sinatra in an operatic voice. It sends shivers down my spine and goose bumps on my arms. She asks me what I want to do that evening and she rocks my world with her golden and cheerful voice. She gets my **interest** because I was bored and now she has my undivided attention.

Since I think in terms of instant reciprocity with my wife, I have to pay her back in the same day; especially as she appeals to my needs. I remembered she told me last week that she was craving butter scotch ice cream. Even though I had no intentions of going out, I consider leaving the house because of my love for her. I realize that I need to make a **decision**, so I get dressed and take her out because I want to impress her with the succulent butter scotch ice cream.

I go to the ice cream parlor and we start savoring the moment as we both dedicated our night to the mission. I talk to the clerk and he claims that he ran out of butter scotch, but he is more than willing to make more. This will take thirty minutes. Since I love my wife so much, I prove it by waiting for her butter scotch ice cream to be prepared. She stated that it would be acceptable that she gets cookies and cream, but she says this in order to see if I really love her (she always tests my love!). I took her into my arms and comforted her in the cold ice cream parlor. I sing her sweet lullabies to prepare her for what is about to arrive. The ice cream is delivered and we indulge like it was our wedding cake. This is the **action** I take. My wife loves me and I love her too!

You have seen how the A.I.D.A. model works. Let me share an example of how the billion-dollar, Fortune 500 companies use this technique. You have seen hundreds, maybe even thousands of television commercials before that have used A.I.D.A. to win you over to their products or services. They use attention-grabbing devices to get you pasted onto the television screen. These words, phrases, and actions entice you to buy. It is difficult for most of us to turn off an attractive beer commercial endorsed by big-time celebrity, or a Mercedes-Benz commercial that takes a scenic drive through the city in top-notch status.

Take the example of a McDonald's television commercial. If you live in America, I am assuming that you have seen one before. They start their commercials off dramatically by playing some of hypnotizing music. The music may generate nostalgia. It may take you back to a memory and you may be emotional in some way. Now, they have both your **attention** and your **interest** simultaneously in the first 5-7 seconds. That is why they are very effective. They will allow you to feel the results buying their products will generate. They are not selling the product itself; they are actually selling the result of the product.

Next, a Big Mac flies across the screen looking as robust as a burger can look. The lettuce and tomatoes are hanging off the edge with crispy fries as its accomplice. The sauce creeps off the side for the sauce-lovers. The burger lands into the hands of a pulchritudinous young woman in the park. She has the look of complete pleasure in her seductive eyes as an entire squad of male basketball players walk by wishing that they could get a bite of her burger. McDonald's is selling happiness, comfort, and even relationships. Are you going to buy it? You will if you want to be happy, comfortable, and in a good-standing relationship with your friend.

This pressure may not get you at that moment, but the next time you are hungry and you pass golden arch on the way home, it will make you think about that commercial, whether it is consciously or unconsciously. You will have a **decision** to make either way. Subconsciously, we make ourselves feel hungry by allowing the television commercial to seep into our minds. The decision can be made in the moment or later when you are confronted with a McDonald's. When you pass the golden arch, you will not think of the commercial you saw a day or two ago. You will be conflicted with supplementing your happiness by ordering in the drive-thru. Consciously, the choice is yours to go for the burger or not.

No matter how much people try to avoid fast food, many get caught up in the advertising. Even if you ate one hour ago, you are still going to ask yourself, "Am I hungry?" If you succumb to the pressure of the television commercial, you will tell yourself, "It's time for a burger right now!" You will feel like it is time to indulge on a burger because of the television commercial. Is the hungriness that we have for food or is it the potential to be happy? This is a great question we need to ask.

Let's say you are hungry and you choose to eat what you have in your house. You go for the lean broccoli, carrots, and broiled fish. You take **action** by standing up to the force of the McDonald's commercial that comes across your screen. Even though it takes time to prepare a worthy meal, you know to yourself that you have done the right thing and did not disobey your mind. In the long run, the action you take will have consequences. It doesn't matter what you do because the consequences will be inevitable, whether you go for the home-cooked dinner or the Big Mac and fries.

Obviously, if you were to let the television commercial affect the way you think, you will find that you will be heading to the golden arch and you will be feasting on a juicy burger in no time. The Big Mac would then tell you that you are not happy if you realize that it has gotten you to buy it because of your own weakness. You were sold to! Although you may wipe off the pain temporarily, it will catch up to you and it could be difficult to prevent the temptation the next time you see a television commercial.

You have seen how AIDA works. When you are selling a product or service, you are actually selling the result or the perceived result of that product or service. When you are selling life insurance, you are selling personal security for yourself and your family. When you are selling mortgages, you are selling financial convenience. When you are selling real estate, you are selling dreams. When you give people what they want in an honest way, they will trust you and buy from you if you are willing to appeal to their needs. If you learn how to use A.I.D.A., you will find that it can be applicable in anything you do. You will also be able to resist being sold to in the marketplace. Stand up to the pressures of consumerism and handle it the way you know you should. Just remember, You are the Boss!

9

Relationships

"We make a living by what we get, but we make a life by what we give." - Winston Churchill

As you may already know, the pursuit of a relationship is one of the primary objectives of every living creature. If you never had anyone your life, your loneliness would be inexpressible. All people have unique gifts, talents, and abilities that they may render to help other people. You have something that I will never have and I have something that you will never have. If we become friends, we can share our blessings. Relationships are the glue that holds people together. People benefit from others every day. People are continually sharing and they are committed to helping others every day. When you are down, you should call up to someone who could sooth you. When you are up, you should always reach down to someone who is not as high as you are. Relationships are the exponents by which we foster each other's growth. Just as iron sharpens iron, we can enhance each other's unique qualities by having the right relationships. In this chapter, I will cover a variety of relationships that people may have.

The Master Mind Principle

What is a Master Mind? It is the embodiment of people with complementary gifts, skills, and experiences. With the accumulation of one mind, you will be able to target bigger goals than you would be able to if you were by yourself. Napoleon Hill, the man who has helped more self-made millionaires than any living person defines a Master Mind as, "The coordination of knowledge and effort, in a spirit of harmony, between two or more people, for the attainment of a definite purpose." No one can do anything outstanding without the Master Mind principle. It is the fastest way for people to grow. No person can grow alone; we need people to help us make changes.

With this principle, you will gain the perspective, advice, and counsel of others. The availability of your constituents in your Master Mind will help you clarify your thinking, and will promote the best decisions. Have you ever had a decision to make and realized that it needed to go to someone else to help you decide before taking further action? If the person you have chosen to help is sensible, they will be able to detect the pitfalls and dangers that may lie ahead. At the same time, they will be able to pour ideas to help further the plan if your decision is a good choice.

What about the contrary? Have you ever had a decision to make and you didn't choose to go to someone knowing you should have? Many decisions without proper council can end in disaster. There might have been a reasonable solution to your problem that could have been easily detected by utilizing your friends. By doing this, you will make fewer mistakes.

Jesus was an excellent use of this principle. He had twelve trusted disciples. They all asked different questions because they always sought to understand life's problems more clearly. The Bible states that they were very different from each other and were assigned different positions because of this. They were harmonious men, until Judas, the Betrayer, left the group. They solved all kinds of problems and were able to explore the miracles that were performed by Jesus, who was their leader. Because of the Master Mind of the twelve disciples, Jesus was able to carry out His mission to go to Jerusalem while healing and teaching many people along the way. The Bible goes very deeply into the Master Mind principle.

Great pioneers need Master Minds too. When a big business or organization is established, they need attorneys, accountants, secretaries, drivers, chefs, advisors, construction worker, managers, and specialists. They must also be cooperative and trustworthy in the business. Team work makes the dream work. Without the proper helpers, nothing great can be established.

Let's take the example of a high school. Any school needs teachers who specialize in the core subjects of Social Studies, Science, Math, and English. The school also needs janitors, librarians, crossing guards, cafeteria workers, principals, technicians, and administrators to keep the facilities running efficiently. It's hard for any institution to succeed without the help of committed individuals who are focused on achieving the same objectives. The Master Mind principle is the strongest way to get to where you need to go. If you have ever studied any historic leaders in the past, such as: Henry Ford, Andrew Carnegie, Steve Jobs, Bill Gates, or

Abraham Lincoln, you understand that they become the individuals they were because of their commitment to the Master Mind principle. Try to find the right people who fit on your team. Your dreams will happen when you surround yourself with people who want to explore the same objectives as you do.

Competition

I will argue the pros and cons of competition for you to decide where you want to be.

Most people do not realize how deleterious competition can actually be. When we fight with others instead of making them our allies, we defeat ourselves. In fact, the most formidable opponent you may ever face is the person in the mirror. We often cheat ourselves by thinking we can get ahead of others. We should be focusing on becoming our best selves, not being better than someone else. It is impossible to have dominion over someone and choose what is best for them. Competition makes us use our will wrongfully. Often times, when we have a conflict with our enemy, we can stir up hate in the process and there may be unintended consequences in the process. People who are involved may also get hurt as well. Instead, we should turn our adversaries into friends. You learn and gain more from them that way.

"A merchant who approaches business with the idea of serving the public well has nothing to fear from the competition."
- J. C. Penney

We live in a world that is full of abundance. There is way too much to be fighting over one piece of bread. Since most people think in terms of scarcity, this causes them to fight. Scarcity creates more value because more people want the resources that are less readily available. People compete for exclusivity. Thousands of men and women want the highly esteemed title of being the President of the United States of America. There can only be one in every 4-8 years and people compete for the position. However, if a person wanted to be the mayor of a town or a city, and some other type of electoral position, the availability would be wide open.

If you create a path that was unexplored, there would obviously be no competition. After Mark Zuckerberg created Facebook by utilizing the Master Mind principle, many people doubted its validity or future success. Others claimed that they would have made the same thing if they had the same opportunity as Zuckerberg. Nowadays, everyone is competing for "likes" and "comments" on the social media platform he has created. Others are creating social media that can gain similar attention like Facebook. Linkedin is a great example of this.

What is good about competition? Businesses do shave off costs for the consumers when competition is in town. We are able to get great prices on vehicles because there are so many companies that compete in the marketplace. Competition demands the best possible effort from every individual and industry as a whole. Isn't it true that an average person will start to put above-average work into what they are doing once they find themselves in competition? Don't we thrive on competition? Many Americans believe that competition helps us grow.

Competition is meaningful to many and it helps them compete for something that is worthwhile. If a sales department is always competing to be the first to sell one million units, that can be viewed as good competition because it allows you to exert more than you thought you could. Competition is similar to the Master Mind principle in some ways, in that it allows people to work together for a common good, but also for their individual gain or benefit. People will help each other out in competition and can grow because of it. However, this is not always the case because people have a tendency to get envious of other people's successes. Competition must be handled properly. If it isn't it can backfire and cause great harm to even the most momentous individuals and industries.

Competition is an exhibition that could be construed in order that certain people will not fit. For instance, when a short man walks into an NBA game, he knows that it is unlikely he could ever play in a game because of how much competition he sees before him. This means that he will most likely put no effort because he knows that being a basketball player on the NBA court is not in his favor. Conversely, it may get that man focused on what he could be doing best once he sees the diligence of being an athlete. He may become motivated because of this. I believe that the Olympics are the highest form of competition. There are many athletes in the world, but only one will come out victorious. Athletes train for years and pour out their heart and soul into their training, but may still lose because of their formidable competition.

Direct competition leaves little room for creation. Most people are searching for ways to make something that already exist even better. In fact, it may be easier to create something entirely new. Instead of focusing all of your efforts on improving something that already exist, it may make more sense to come up with something useful that no one has ever heard about. You may be trying to concoct the perfect peanut butter, but what if you could create almond butter? It might be easier and taste better!

Competition has the potential to be good or bad, depending on who and where you are. Competition can make you work harder for the things you want or it can hurt you by placing you in a situation that doesn't favor your strengths. You will have stronger mindset if you compete for something worthwhile. Decide for yourself if you want to compete or create. You can also do both, for competition can help you create, and creating can help you compete. The choice is yours. You are the Boss!

Real-Lationships

Since we were discussing social media before, we might as well enter the sphere of actual friendships. Practically everyone has a social media site. People are going to fewer meetings, reading fewer books, and investing less time with real friends. I was heavily involved in social media when it first became popular in the early 2000's, I remember how many 'friends' I had. I realized that these were only virtual representations of friends and that if had few to none in real life. Once I relinquished all social media for an entire year, I found myself making 'actual' friendships among people I can relate to with all five of my senses. It felt better to be around real people rather than communicating with multiple personalities behind a computer screen.

Today, people think about quantity of friends more than quality of friends. Although it is good to have many friends, we should pay attention to the kind of people we are keeping around. Some people carry heavy burdens with them and they can slow you down. Because we are so dynamic, people with problems will come to you and ask for your assistance in solving their issues. It is best to stay away from people who bring you their problems as a means to maintaining their relationship, especially when there is no benefit to you.

The better kind of people can bless you in many ways. The exchange of problems and solutions are not only mutual, but incompatible. To keep virtuous friends, you need to have something good to offer and be able to offer it willingly. Reciprocity always makes its rounds. You will reap what you sow..

Always find out how a person is willing and able to be reached. If you choose to call when your friend prefer to text only, you can have a real dilemma. There are still some people who do not text or send emails. Thankfully, there are really flexible people who are willing to adapt to the new ways of living. Do not be a dinosaur and not adopt any of it. You also don't want to be the kind of person who is a 'slave' to the phone. It is easy to catch people texting under any circumstances. People text in the shower, while cooking, driving, studying, running, and even in a conversation with another person! If you are someone who does this, you may want to reconsider your actions for the benefit of your interaction. Friends are very important, but if they are demanding you to respond as quickly as you can all of the time, it may be best to lose them. Today, both texting and social media have become the biggest form of learning among people. The majority of people find their information by these methods of communication.

"The information you get from social media is not a substitute for academic discipline at all."
-Bill Nye

WIIFM

Everyone is tuned into their favorite station, 'WIIFM,' or 'What's In It For Me?' People always want to know how you can help them; otherwise, you might as well not inquire about being their friend. If you become a friend first, your list of friends will be endless. If you are waiting for someone to talk to you, most likely only a few will approach you. Have something good to offer. Make sure to always approach people with love and understanding. Be aware of the reactions of the person you are befriending. If they say something or their body indicates a certain emotion, try to understand their emotion and logic behind it.

Studying a good gesture book and talking to more people will help you ascertain peoples' emotions and behaviors. Alan Pease describes body language in many of his books and videos. He emphasizes that you should never exclude people in conversations and form cliques by your body language. You wouldn't want someone to ever do it to you. Seek first to understand and always be willing to listen to others. If you give your full attention, people will be more inclined to give you anything they are capable of giving. People always think about themselves, and if you know how to cater to them in the right way, at the right time, with the right tone, you can reach them faster than a hungry man at the buffet line. They will give you anything if you fully offer your service. In short, people will tell you everything they need, whether it is verbal or non-verbal. If you can pick up the cues and deliver, they will tune into your station: "WCIDFY" or 'What Can I Do for You?" Be sure to always approach people with the willingness and readiness to serve to their needs.

"If you help enough people get what they want,
you will get what you want." - Zig Ziglar

The 'Right' People

Since we all have something good to offer, we may not realize that we need to market ourselves. Marketing is instrumental if you want to build your business, relationships, church, or any institution or endeavor. If you are a good actress, you may not be as successful in rural areas as you would be in urban areas. If you are a good writer, but you never submit your works to newspapers, magazines, etc., you may never get the exposure you need. If you want to sell luxury products, but you live in lower income areas, you need to find a way to do so. Find your niche and deliver the service to the right people.

Currently you may be the kind of person who lives in a place where you cannot grow into the person that you want to become. With proper planning a pen and a dream, you can remove yourself from that environment. I have seen hundreds of men and women who have undervalued themselves by settling in a place or an occupation they didn't truly want. Some ended up in small places when they should have been shouting from the balconies of a big city.

If you have a major mindset and a vision, being in the wrong location can be a major setback. You may have a panoramic vision, but when you wake up, you find yourself with those of myopic vision. If you aren't where you hope to be within the next 3-5 years, there is a very high chance that your dreams will be shutdown. Nature plays no games with the person who doesn't really want to grow. Position yourself for success by aggressively pursuing growth among the right people who can help you reach your dreams.

Make the right decision and take your seed to fertile land where you can flourish and bear the fruit you have always wanted. You will certainly find friends who can nourish you in the process of your development. You can grow exponentially within the next 3-5 years when you take the noteworthy prescription. Otherwise, you are doomed to failure and will rot with the people who cannot help you. Never conform to your environment when you can customize one that is ideal to your needs and functionalities. Everyone will profit because of your decision of surrounding yourself with the right people. When the majority of the stream is going one way, go the completely opposite way. Excellence is calling you my friend. Adhere to the truth of that statement.

"Excellence is the best deterrent to adversity."
-Daniel Ally

We Are the Same People

As I have traveled to many places in the world, I realize that people are the same wherever you go. There will always be someone helpful. There will always be someone who despises you. There will always be those who are rich and poor. There will always be someone who has profound wisdom and insight about life. There is always someone around who will be your tour guide. Someone will always embrace you with love and respect. People are similar wherever you go. Go out there and acquire new friendships. If you learn a new language and/or live in an unfamiliar culture, the more you can relate to a new type of lifestyle. When I went to China, all I needed was a few Mandarin Chinese expressions to help me communicate effectively. It helped me get into a few doors!

People want the same things in life. They want to be happy and healthy. They want to have a healthy family with plenty of food and a suitable place to live. A wise man once told me that "wisdom is knowing that we are all the same." Many people prefer to see differences, but in reality, we are all the same. The more you understand this, the wiser you will be. You will be able to love people tirelessly when you see that we are all related. Treat everyone as your siblings, parents, and children—depending on the situation. You will far in life once you adopt this powerful mindset. You will be treated like family everywhere you go when you make yourself a part of other's extended family. This is love in its highest regard. We are all family!

Dating and Marriage

I am surprised how many people struggle to find intimacy with others. I must admit that I got more dating offers when I started to dress better, got smarter, and earned money. That's not the only way to find a date however. In my opinion, the easiest way to find the best person for you is to search in a place where you think there would be someone similar to you in all personality, spiritual, and occupational qualities.

I have seen men and women go to bars because they think that it is the best place to meet quality people. Instead, why not find a date at church, work, school, or the gym? The key is to get out there and know what you are looking for. You must be willing to engage in purposeful discussions and be able to discuss a variety of topics. You must also be real and genuine with everyone you meet. Dating sites and social media websites are other useful options. There are many dating sites and social media websites that can help you find a quality relationship. I have known people who have found their spouses that way. Before you get ahead of yourself and talk about marriage or living together, make sure you ask hardball questions and talk about financials such as debt, additional income, allocation of expenses, and any other monetary questions. Some couples get married and soon find out that their spouse has six-figure debt and a spendthrift mindset. Money is the greatest divider among relationships. Marriage is the leading cause of divorce. Don't marry the wrong people and never rush into a marriage.

Most marriages fail because there is a lack of trust, a sense of boredom, or because there are financial difficulties. It also fails because the couple may not understand each other. All it takes to maintain any marriage is creativity and diligence in appealing to each other's needs. Marriage is not a contract, but a covenant. It should not be transactional, but eternal. Never try to force an emotion, a feeling, or a circumstance to occur that is not there in the relationship. The worse thing that can happen is when two people marry each other for the wrong reasons or forcing a marriage that isn't quite ready. Abstain from sex until you are married. If you are not a virgin and are not married, you should devote yourself wholeheartedly to celibacy. The misuse and abuse of sex leads people into the chamber of death. Also, never try to have a dual relationship. It never works. If you are having an affair in a relationship, quit it immediately. That includes 'sexting' with another person or flirting with others outside of your marriage.

Never burden yourself or your partner because of your indecisiveness. If you are dating someone and are considering marriage, but never got in a real argument, I highly suggest you have one because arguments are inevitable in marriage. If you don't know what to argue about, find something to smooth out in your relationship. Do not be love birds and find out the kind of information that you will regret after you made the wrong decision. You cannot live in an illusion of happiness. Do not assume that everything will work out once you get married. Do some research and discuss the possibility of a future with your partner.

If you are married, be sure to submit to each other fully. Always change up preferences and correspond to each other's needs. Compromise only when necessary. Men and women will be contentious in certain times of the relationship, but this is only to build endurance. In many traditional households, men are the breadwinner in the family. In my opinion, the housewife is the hardest job in the entire planet. Without men and women in their proper roles, I think it causes our society to suffer in inexplicable ways. Since the idea of a family is a controversial topic and many families are diverse, I will leave the family topic alone. If you want one of the best books on the family, I highly suggest "The Christian

Family" by Larry Christenson. It will blow your mind of its practicality and ease of read. If it does not fortify your relationship with your spouse and your family, I do not know what will. God will speak to you directly while you read it. I recommend that you buy it at your earliest convenience.

"A happy family is but an earlier heaven."
-George Bernard Shaw

Passion and Prejudice

The world is filled with passion and prejudice. It is something that we all have in common. When someone is passionate about their job or their religion, it may lead to prejudice toward another person because they do not have the same belief. An inability to find a balance in our minds and lives can lead us to extremes. This imbalance tends to impede into our relationships. A simple change in mindset can alter the way we feel about someone. It is easy to become intensely convicted about our feelings for a person, good or bad. We can join an organization or club and our current friends can become outliers. We can become enthusiastic about cars and anyone who does not like cars cannot become our friends. No one knows why this happens, but it does. Adolf Hitler is a prime example of this. He studied his philosophy to the point where he hated everything that did not agree with it. He even took massive action because he was very passionate in what he believed.

The only way you can guard against this is by knowing your gage of affection toward a person or thing. If you become too infatuated in anything, it may blind you to things that surround you. You may miss opportunities and avoid certain friends. On the contrary, if you become passionate about something that is worthwhile, you may become very good at it and it will attract other people to the kind of work you are able to perform. Whatever it is, know your limit and know how it affects the people around you.

"We must act out passion before we can feel it."- Jean-Paul Sartre

Professional Relationships

Professional relationships are very important if you want to make a significant contribution to society. Sometimes you may lose touch with someone you admire. Hopefully, you will be able to pick up the conversation where it was left off. If not, try to reacquaint yourself with the person you lost touch with. If you are unable to reconnect with the person due to various circumstances, maybe it is time to search for a new relationship. There are professionals readily available to help. The ones who can help you best are the ones who become your friends. Be aware of who you are dealing with at all times. Sometimes a professional friend can also be your secret enemy. You will find that there are all sorts of professionals with different mindsets. That is why it is always good to be well-rounded and flexible in your conversation.

Sometimes you can remember someone by their exact niche. When you think of certain people, their profession automatically comes to mind. For instance, if you heard the name Michael Jordan, the first thing you may think of is basketball. When you think of Steve Jobs, you think of Apple computers, such as the iPod. Usually, if a person is on this kind of professional level where you associate their profession with them, this means that they are most likely successful at what they do. We should all strive for this form of workplace mastery. Being proficient at our work takes years. It is possible when we have the right professional relationships. They can always be developed, no matter who you are. Your network of people will determine your net worth.

Do you know how to gain professional relationships? You can do so by many ways

1. Chamber of Commerce
2. Referrals from other professional friends
3. Linkedin.com
4. Toastmasters International
5. Kiwanis Club
6. Rotary Club
7. Church or other religious institutions
8. Lion’s Club
9. Meetup.com
10. Trade Associations
11. Seminars

12. Airports
13. Restaurants
14. Interviews
15. Gym and Grocery Stores
16. Many more places!

Friends

To conclude, a lot can be said about the subject of relationships. A good measure to check the quality of your friendship is to look at the last five non-family phone calls, emails, and text messages you sent out. If they do not reach the standards you are aiming for, it is time to strategize your new choice of friends. Be sure of who your friends are. Sometimes an enemy can appear to be a friend. There are many people who seem to be your friends, but they are not. It reminds me of the old story about the 'Scorpion and the Frog.' A scorpion and a frog meet on the bank of a stream and the scorpion asks the frog to carry him across on its back. The frog asks, "How do I know you won't sting me?" The scorpion says, "Because if I do, I will die too." The frog reasons with the scorpion and agrees with his logic, and they set out, but while swimming midstream, the scorpion stings the frog. In great disbelief, the frog feels the onset of paralysis and starts to sink, knowing they both will drown, but has just enough time to gasp "Why?" The scorpion replies, "It's my nature..."

I advise you to surround yourself with people who will help you grow. If you want to succeed in life, be sure to be around people who are smarter and better than you. Get around people who have done what you want to do. Always put yourself in a position where you can help and are open to be helped. There are many places that can nurture your growth and help you to be in the right place at the right time. Never put yourself in unnatural positions or groups of people where you know you will never fit. If it feels right, do it. Opportunity will visit you frequently once you begin to recognize that your relationships you hold make the difference. After all, my last name is 'Ally' and I am a friend you can trust because I love you. Love is a verb. Love your friends and your enemies because You are the Boss!

"Friends and good manners will carry you where money won't go." - Margaret Walker

10

Faith

"Faith begins as an experiment and ends as an experience."

- William Ralph Inge

In this world, in order to move mountains of any sorts, we need faith. Everything we do requires faith. You have reached this chapter of this book because you have faith that it will get better as read. Faith is the substance of things hoped for, the evidence of things unseen. This means that everything you hoped for will come to fruition as long as you believe. You will also have to be diligent as you work in faith. Having faith requires action. Positive action mixed with positive faith leads to positive results. It makes sense to execute these results by faith because there is no sense just playing it safe. Walk in faith, not by sight.

Faith demands the use of imagination, desires, and fantasies. Do you believe that you have the faith necessary to achieve the goals in your life? Everyone possesses a unique gift inside them which is predestined to help them succeed. Perhaps it may be a gift in music, or one in cooking. Maybe it is one in writing, or one in speaking. You may have a gift of patience or kindness. You may have an extraordinary gift of self-discipline or self-control. You may have a gift of persuasion. There could be technical gifts, or counseling gifts. Maybe you ask questions, or you can be a provocative thinker. Your gift could be in teaching, humor, or mere intelligence. You could have a gift in discerning mechanical equipment or understanding languages. You might have a gift of preaching. You may even be physically gifted with strength or flexibility. No matter who you are, you have at least one gift that has been endowed to you. You must use this gift to creatively express yourself. When you do, you will gain more faith in the process.The main point is that there are many gifts and it takes much faith to activate them. All of us have faith, but faith is useless unless it comes out of us and is used for a greater purpose.

One of my favorite stories is the one of Colonel Harland David Sanders. If the name sounds familiar, it is! He is the man who you see at many KFC's across the United States of America, and now in various countries. His story fascinates me because it is one of pure faith, even at a late age. From his 1974 autobiography, he was born in Henryville, Indiana in 1890. Six years later, his father died, forcing his mother to enter the workforce to support the family. At the ripe age of six, young Harland was responsible for taking care of his younger siblings and doing the majority of the family's cooking. In just a few years, he was able to master several eventually famous recipes.

Before Harland Sanders became a world-famous Colonel, he was a sixth-grade dropout, a farmhand, an army mule-tender, a locomotive fireman, a railroad worker, an aspiring lawyer, an insurance salesman, a ferryboat entrepreneur, a tire salesman, an amateur obstetrician, an unsuccessful political candidate, a gas station operator, a motel operator and eventually, a restaurateur.

Although Colonel Sanders worked all kinds of odd-jobs for the next 30 years, he found himself in a position to keep up with his culinary skills. In 1930, the then 40-year-old Sanders operated a service station in Corbin, Kentucky. It was there that he began cooking for hungry travelers who stopped in for gas. He didn't have a restaurant yet, so patrons ate from his own dining table in the station's humble living quarters. It was during this time that he invented what's called "home meal replacement" — selling complete meals to busy, time-strapped families. He called it, "Sunday Dinner, Seven Days a Week." As Sanders' fame grew, Governor Ruby Laffoon made him a Kentucky Colonel in 1935 in recognition of his contributions to the state's cuisine. Within four years, his establishment was listed in Duncan Hines' "Adventures in Good Eating." It wasn't' long after that people started visiting strictly for the food (instead of the gas). Colonel Sanders had to move across the street to accommodate his increasing dining capacity.

At the age of 65, his small business in Corbin, Kentucky was taken away because a route alteration on Interstate 75. The restaurant Sanders established was abandoned and he was left with nothing but a Social Security check and a secret recipe for fried chicken. This was enough for the Colonel Sanders to apply his faith and gift. Over the next decade, he perfected his secret blend of 11 herbs and spices with a basic cooking technique which is being still used today. In 1955, confident of the quality of his fried chicken, the Colonel devoted himself to developing his chicken franchising business. He knocked on thousands of doors across America and slept in his car for many nights. There were several occasions where he had to bathe in the sink of public bathrooms. All of this was in pursuit of his dream. Less than 10 years later, Sanders had more than 600 KFC franchises in the U.S. and Canada. In 1964, he sold his interest in the U.S. company for $2 million to a group of investors including John Y. Brown Jr. (who later became the governor of Kentucky). Up until he was fatally stricken with leukemia in 1980 at the age of 90, the Colonel traveled 250,000 miles a year visiting KFC restaurants around the world. His likeness continues to appear on millions of buckets and on thousands of restaurants in more than 100 countries around the world. This is very ambitious for a man who started from absolutely nothing at an age most people consider their retirement years. He transmuted his faith and overcame a lot of adversity in the process of growing KFC.

"Be faithful in small things because it is in them that your strength lies." - Mother Theresa

Just like Colonel Sanders, once an ordinary man, you can gain tremendous success in any endeavor in the world when you have the desire to act. You need a plan of action and faith to succeed. Often times, when I travel to other states or outside of the country, I need a lot of faith because I am extending beyond my comfort zone. One day, I realized that when I do what I have never done before, go places where I have never been, and I am able to try something new, I find myself in deep prayer and hopes that we will be able to make the best of the opportunity as it presents itself. Because I have faith, I take comfort in all I do, say, and feel because I know there is a purpose behind my action. An old philosopher said, "Faith is not knowing what the future holds, but who holds the future." Do you have faith in your future?

In order to gain and sustain your faith, you have to remember what you have done to get you where you stand today. You are either in a place where you want to be, or a place where you do not want to be. All you have to do is choose to follow the path of your destiny and find the best way to get to what you desire. It does not matter where you are now; all that matters is where you plan to go. After you decide where you want to go, create plans whereby you can draw up blueprints to take deliberate action step to your intended destination. Remember the 5 P's? Proper Planning Prevents Poor Performance.

In due time, you will find yourself in the place you always wanted to be. Continue to have faith and you will advance to better places. All you have to do is take the same step of faith to lead yourself in the direction just as you have before. By faith, success is a habit that can be highly attainable. Faith is the nourishment that sustains you. It will relieve anxiety and any kind of discouragement that you may be conflicted with. Faith will set you free when you believe in yourself and the Higher Power.

Someone once said that if you "feed your faith, your fears will starve to death." Read that again. Someone else said "faith is the continuation of reason." The great Martin Luther King Jr. said; "Take the first step in faith. You don't have to see the whole staircase, just take the first step." That is all you have to do, take the first step when you have a mature plan of action and everything will work itself out, even though it may be challenging.

"You cannot have faith when you have doubt. You cannot doubt when you have faith."-Daniel Ally

Faith and happiness are correlated. Faith helps you get the things that you want. Happiness helps you want the things that you get. Have you ever waited for someone for a long time and finally see them come? Well you had faith. Do you remember how that made you feel? Did you feel happy? There is no doubt. In contrast, have you ever seen someone who had no faith in their team at a baseball game? They kept saying "We're going to lose," "We're never going to win," and "Our team is trash." What do you think happens when their team loses? The person with no faith becomes unhappy, as if they never could have expected the unfortunate outcome of losing. There are many people who have no faith in themselves, no faith in their work, and no faith in the world. Can you imagine what would happen if we could gain more faith in all of life's circumstances? Our predicaments would automatically become far better than we had hoped. Sometimes, all you need is faith. I know you will have more faith.

There is a quote that says, "I thought I had it bad when I had no shoes, until I saw someone with no feet!" Most people are happy when they have faith in an outcome or circumstance that they believe will be favorable. Whatever you believe in, believe in it wholeheartedly. There is no sense in having faith in something you believe you can never have faith in. People who have no faith begin to discourage others because they cannot do or believe in what is happening. The person with faith will encourage others, because they know that they will do something beneficial to society. Never live a half-hearted life. It will do well for no one.

Both encouragement and discouragement are pervasive. Your worst enemy is discouragement, which is lack of faith. Your best friend is encouragement, which is full of faith. Many people do not have faith because they think in terms of scarcity. They believe that there isn't enough faith to go around. You should know that we do not need to compete for the same pie; rather, we must create a larger one. And it begins by having more faith. You must have faith that there is actually a bigger pie out there, just like Colonel Harland Sanders did. Will you have more faith today?

Many times our faith can be challenged by our circumstances and exterior forces. Sometimes we feel that people and circumstances may become obstacles in our lives. We are often mentally and physically drained from the demands of our jobs or perhaps there may be a spoiled apple in your life. Willie Jolley said, "A setback is nothing but a setup for a comeback." Is there someone stopping you? Don't let one of these challenges prevent you from reaching the fulfillment of your desires. This is where faith can come into play and change your perspective completely when you use it correctly.

Have you ever seen someone who loses their mind after a series of life issues? The person who struggles and loses their mind doesn't have faith. You must be able to face the issues that stand in your way. The issues and circumstances of life will eventually see the positive side. Do not let circumstances or exterior forces prohibit them from being happy. You must be baptized with faith and carry it everywhere you go. Let your faith be felt when you walk the Earth.

Here are twelve simple suggestions to gaining more faith:

1. Carry your goals with you everywhere you go.
2. Have a trustworthy confidant who you can go to for advice.
3. Read inspiring literature before you start your day (example: The Bible).
4. Challenge your faith by getting outside of your comfort zone.
5. Remove yourself from negative environments in which no growth takes place.
6. Begin to take serious steps in building your character.
7. Attend lectures, seminars, classes, and panels.
8. Listen to audio programs on your commute or while participating in daily activities.
9. Read one or more inspirational quotes per day.
10. Pray as often as you can.
11. Befriend individuals who are like-minded in their faith.
12. Make affirmations that you know are true.

The last suggestion, making affirmations is very important. Self-talk, or affirmations, has the potential to promote your confidence in yourself and your faith.

For instance:

"I am the best piano player."
"I am good at sales."
"I am stronger."
"Each and every day, in every way, I am getting better and better."
"Today is going to be the best day of my life."
"People need my products and services."
"I am going to be the best at what I do."
"I am going to make it."
"I can feel myself growing."
"God is always good."
"I love people."
"I am intelligent."
"People need more because I serve them well."

These types of affirmations will begin to seep into your subconscious mind and take you to a deeper level of thinking. When you do recite these types of phrases every day, you will begin to see a difference in your mindset. They will always help you if you do them the right way consistently. This is called auto-suggestion because you are suggesting to yourself anything you want to take place in your life. It works all the time. You must set reminders to consistently make these affirmations. Post sticky notes, write on white boards, and set yourself up with these affirmations everywhere in your house, car, and work. Talk with your confidant and affirm each other in these ways too.

"Relentless, repetitive self-talk is what changes our self-image."
-Denis Waitley

Faith can be developed when you take the right actions and believe in your dreams. Nourish your faith daily to live happily. Faith begins with trusting yourself, other people, and God. When you can trust everyone, yourself, and the Higher Power, you will find that anything noteworthy in your life can be accomplished as long as you have faith. Try rehearsing your own suggestions today and see which ones will take you to a higher level of faith. Start with, "I feel happy, I feel healthy, and I feel terrific!!" You will find yourself in places where you never knew you could have been. Faith sees the invisible, believes the incredible, and receives the impossible.

Believe in yourself and the Almighty God. Believe in the systems and structures of your work and government. Mingle with people who believe in you and themselves. Many people do not believe because of the subtle influences of the people around them. The best way I gain faith for myself is by praising God for all the opportunities that He gave me. I thank Him for making me who I am today and for helping me understand myself and others. You are the

Boss when you have more faith! God can help you expand your faith when you believe in Him.

"What shall we say about such wonderful things?
If God is for us, who can ever be against us?"
-Romans 8:31 (New Living Translation)

11
Money

"The lack of money is the root of all evil." -Mark Twain

Money is very important. A nation's balance amongst its people or with other nation's tends to be strongly gauged on its currency and overall monetary stability in contributing to international trade. It is the circulating medium of exchange. Without it, there would be more bloodshed than ever before. Earlier in the book, we discussed how it replaced the bartering system. In the same way, money creates peace, which is highly contrary to popular beliefs. Money can help solve a lot of the world problems if only it were used in the right ways. There is never a shortage of money. People seem to think that they are only worth a certain amount of money per hour or per year, but they are forcing limitations on themselves. In the United States of America, many individuals have the potential to become a millionaire, if that is what they truly desire.

The rapper, Biggie Smalls, had a song called "Mo' Money, Mo' Problems." It is true. The acquisition and retention of money comes with many challenges. These challenges are good. It means that you are engaging in commerce and in doing this, love and money is the byproduct. The popular mindset among many Americans is that "money is the root of all evil." The Bible verse in 1st Timothy 6:10 actually revealed, "The LOVE of money is the root of all evil." There is a big difference between those two statements. Money is neither good nor bad. It doesn't have emotions. Would you call a car good or bad? What about a sofa?

I am sure you have heard your parents, relatives or friends say, "Money doesn't grow on trees." Or "Money doesn't buy happiness." Or "Save for a rainy day." Or "That's too expensive." Or "This is hard-earned, back-breaking money." These poor philosophies can be painful because money is one of the most replaceable things in the world. What most people do not realize is that there is an abundance of money. Many jobs pay you just enough to keep you alive. If you need $4,000 per month to live, your job will give you $4,500 to make you feel good. If you get a raise, your standard of living will raise too. This doesn't mean that you will have much money unless you become highly specialized in an industry, work as a salesperson, or own your own business.

Many people tend to believe poor philosophies because they do not understand the fundamentals of money. They do not comprehend that money is acquired by rendering useful and creative services. People wake up thinking that they are going to their 40 hour-per-week jobs (or 9-5 pm) and that they will make $20 per hour. It's assumed that they will have a gross income of $140 for the day. Unfortunately, the exchange of time for money is the worst exchange known to humankind. You can always replace money, but you can't replace time.

It causes frustration and prevents people from fully actualizing their meaningful purpose in life. Although, there are some 9-5 pm jobs where people are truly happy with what they do and actually obtain their 'money's worth,' please recognize that this is not true for the majority of Americans. There are some people who can be working on their dreams instead of the jobs they do not prefer to work at. What is even worse about this is that they will take on other part-time jobs that they don't like. They end up working 60-80 hours at jobs that kill them. This is where life can beat most people up.

Many people are unsatisfied with their financial position and they fail to do anything about their disposition. The honest elementary school teacher, engineer, and nurse may by living their dreams in their 9-5 pm routines. Meanwhile, a woman who is a secretary for her piggish boss or the man, who works 70 hours per week at a car dealership in a highly competitive and cutthroat atmosphere, suffers inexplicably. It is especially true if they are underpaid for what the work they do not enjoy. There are many restaurant worker who easily put 40-60 hours on the job and yet barely have enough money to survive. This is even worse when the person knows that they could be doing better, but instead never takes the initiative or makes the necessary plans and strategies. JOB stands for 'Just Over Broke.' However, not all people who have jobs are broke, but most of them are. I found this out after working over my observation in while working over thirty jobs.

Many seem to be content on the benefits that their job gives them. They build up a 'golden nest' their whole life only to find out that they cannot enjoy it once they reach the age where they can tap into their social security fund. This is the equivalent of 'putting all of your eggs in one basket.' Today, many people are working well into their 60's, 70's, 80's, and in some cases 90's. This is tragic especially when no one is willing or able to work at that age. Many individuals do not know what to do with their money because they never took the time to study it or attend a class/seminar. There is little to no financial education taught in homes, schools, churches, or work. Many people just earn it and burn it. Others save and seldom enjoy it. These are two extreme philosophies that clearly show that most people are always worried about money.

Often people neglect to research accordingly prior to reaching this age and then they hold contempt for anyone who moves through life successfully. There are many people in their 40's or 50's who wonder how another person in their 20's earn twice as much money as them. I know many people who think that financially successful people 'sold themselves to the devil' or 'slept with his/her boss' to make it, however I know that most of the accused people did have a modest and ethical plan to attain their financial status. No one can succeed financially and feel good about themselves while harming people. I have met many charlatans who put up false claims of what they can do, but rarely do I see them deliver. There are also people who promote sex, drugs, and violence, but their justice is served and their paths will come to a horrific ending.

People study various subjects, like sports and news, but money is the last thing that they feel they should learn. They know all the stats from the NFL, NBA, NHL, and MLB, but if you check their financial statements, you'll find that most of them are broke. Many Americans fill their minds with many infinitesimal things and they never even put a thought into their financial situation. People will plan a party for two months, but will never pick up a book on money. The thought of money is an insidious thing and their relation with it is toxic. Many people should master money, instead of letting money master them.

"Money is a terrible master but an excellent servant."
–P.T. Barnum

There is an economic theory called a 'zero-sum game.' This theory basically states that if they obtain money from another person, they will win and the other person will lose. Many people will not go after money because they think that they will hurt others in the process. Many business owners will undercharge their clients because they don't want the other person to feel bad. Most people seek approval and they feel that if they get money from others, they will lose their friendship. Conversely, if you exchange money with others, you are engaging in love and commerce. More money is created and everyone is benefited. If you have a worthwhile product or service, it is best that you charge a fair price for it. You will not be hurting the other person; you will be helping them by providing a solution to make their life easier. Money is the exchange for the solution that you offer. The zero-sum game is a major reason why people do not accumulate money.

"Fortune sides with him who dares." –Virgil

Money can do a lot of things. It can even make people go crazy. If you ever dropped a dollar bill in the mall and left it there, you will find people scrambling for it and some will even treat it as if it was their best day ever. If you haven't tried this before, it is amusing to see. It will not hurt anyone if you try it. While it is true that people think about money a lot, it is also true that they do not have the right thoughts about it. You will find that it is true in this experiment.

Growing up in New York City, I have seen people do all sorts of things for money. For a long time, I have wanted to give away millions of dollars and create soup kitchens all over the world. I want to support missionaries programs in churches and donate money to various charity organizations supporting diverse conflicts. I have seen poor families and I have wanted to give them food or help them in any way I could. Although I already do, I want to do it more. There are many ways that you can help without money, but there are more ways that you can help if you have money. In truth, the only way to help poor people is by becoming rich, not by remaining poor.

"Money is just a way of keeping score." - H.L. Hunt

You need to have the proper mindset before you earn money. Without the right mindset, a person will not receive the kind of money and recognition they deserve. There is a lot of money out there and everyone deserves to get a piece of it. There are many ways to earn respectfully by serving people in the right ways. I will share with you some differences in people's mindset. I got this right out of T. Harv Eker's book, "Secrets of the Millionaire Mind." These seventeen files have helped shape my philosophy of earning wealth. I added in my own twist to it. They have taught me the difference between rich and poor people. At the end of each file, he suggests a declaration or affirmation that you can say out loud to enhance a positive mentality.

Wealth File #1:

Rich people believe "I create my life."
Poor people believe "Life happens to me."

When you are complaining, condemning, and comparing with other people you lose much of your money.

Many people are reactive in dealing with people. It is best to be proactive and deal with situations before they arise.

You have complete control over your financial situation every day.

Declaration: "I create the exact level of my financial success!"

Wealth File #2:

Rich people play the money game to win.

Poor people play the money game to not lose.

If your goal is to be comfortable, chances are you'll never get rich. But if your goal is to be rich, chances are you'll end up being mighty comfortable.

"You cannot grow if you are comfortable.
You be comfortable if you do not grow."-Daniel Ally

Declaration: "My goal is to become a millionaire and more!"

Wealth File #3:

Rich people are committed to being rich.

Poor people want to be rich.

The number one reason most people don't get what they want is that they don't know what they want.

If you are not totally and truly committed to creating wealth, chances are you won't.

You must plan your work and work your plan to be as wealthy as you need to be.

Declaration: "I commit to being rich."

Wealth File #4:

Rich people think big.

Poor people think small.

The Law of Income: You will be paid in direct proportion to the value you deliver according to the marketplace.

"You can choose to think in dimes or you can think in dollars."-Daniel Ally

Do you want to earn $100,000 per year or $1,000,000 per year?

Should you charge $40 for your service and deal with amateurs or charge $400 and deal with top-notch professionals?

Will you invest in the best foods and clothing or do you want inferior goods for the rest of your life?

Declaration: "I think big! I choose to help thousands of people!"

Wealth File #5:

Rich people focus on opportunities.

Poor people focus on obstacles.

Are you constantly thinking, "How will I pay the rent this month?" or "How do I find a more luxurious home next year?"

Are you focused on how you can charge your clients less because of their financial situation or are you thinking of how you can build your offering and charge more in order to help them?

Do you look for all the problems in starting or keeping your business or do you look for all of the opportunities to build it?

Declaration: "I focus on opportunities over obstacles."
Declaration: "I get ready, I fire, I aim!"

Wealth File #6:

Rich people admire other rich and successful people.

Poor people resent rich and successful people.

Do you despise the couple in the brand new Mercedes-Benz while you are at the stop light or do you love the fact that they have one and inspired you to get one too?

Are you passing jewelry shops, fancy restaurants, and million-dollar homes and saying, "It's too expensive" and "I can never get that?" Or are you saying, "I am getting that next year." and asking, "What must I do to think like the person I have to become to obtain better goods?"

Test drive your favorite car this week. Visit a home that is ten times past your budget. Order what you want on the menu without looking at the price.

"Bless that which you want." – Huna Philosophy

Declaration: "I admire rich people!"
Declaration: "I bless rich people!"
Declaration: "I love rich people!"
Declaration: "And I am going to be one of those rich people, too!"

Wealth File #7:

Rich people associate with positive and successful people.
Poor people associate with negative or unsuccessful people.

Are the people you are surrounded with helping you or hurting you?

Do your friends help you earn more money or do they constantly ask you for money?

Have you outgrown the groups you are in or do you surround yourself with people who can help you grow?

Would your friends support you if you became rich or will they envy you because of it?

Do you have a wealthy role model(s) who can teach you how to earn and keep money?

Declaration: "I model wealthy and successful people."
Declaration: "I associate with affluent and successful people."
Declaration: "If they can do it, I can do it!"

Wealth File #8:

Rich people are willing to promote themselves and their value. Poor people think negatively about selling and promotion.

Do you persuade people or do you get persuaded by people?

Are you watching someone else live your dream only because you refuse to get out there and offer your product or service at the price you should be demanding from your clients?

Are you an artist, musician, speaker, coach, contractor, consultant, trainer, athlete, doctor, lawyer, engineer, or other kind of practitioner/specialist who earns a fraction of what you can earn because you don't want to sell or promote your services?

Are you waiting on a big promoter to sweep you off your feet by selling and promoting your business or will you take 2-5 years to learn how to do it yourself?

Declaration: "I promote my value to others with passion and enthusiasm."
Declaration: "People enjoy what I have to offer them."
Declaration: "I give people exactly what they want and need."

Wealth File #9:

Rich people are bigger than their problems.
Poor people are smaller than their problems.

The secret to success is not to try to avoid your problems. The secret is to grow yourself so that you are bigger than any problem.

Will you pay for the $2,000 class or seminar to triple or quadruple your income this year and give you lifelong skills?

Are you going to buy the best copier, fax machine, and printer or are you going to keep replacing the ones that don't work consistently?

Are you going to crush your debt today or are you going to let to crush you?

Will you pay for an extra tank of gas or an airplane ticket to attend the event?

"Minimize your problems and maximize your solutions." -Daniel Ally

Declaration: "I am bigger than any problems."
Declaration: "I can handle any problems."

Wealth File #10:

Rich people are excellent receivers.
Poor people are poor receivers.

If you say you're worthy, you are. If you say you're not worthy, you're not. Either way you will live the story you play in your mind.

Do you accept complements about your purse or tie by saying 'thank you' or do you tell them it is 'cheap or old?'

Are you asking people for the business or are you accepting the 'zero-sum game?'

Do you accept when people give you money or do you reject it and tell them to keep it because you are modest or do not need it?

When you reject money, money will reject you.

"If a hundred-foot oak tree had the mind of a human, it would only grow to be ten feet tall!" – T. Harv Eker

For every giver there must be a receiver, and for every receiver there must be a giver.

Money will only make you more of what you already are.

If you tithe 20% of $100,000 every year, you will also tithe 20% of $1,000,000 every year.

Money helps you to express yourself more fully.

Receive and increase steadily. Compounded results over a few years will give you massive success.

How you do anything is how you do everything.

Declaration: "I am an excellent receiver. I am open and willing to receive massive amounts of money into my life."

Wealth File #11:

Rich people choose to get paid based on results.
Poor people choose to get paid based on time.

There's nothing wrong with getting a steady paycheck, unless it interferes with your ability to earn what you're worth. There's the rub. It usually does.

Never have a ceiling on your income.

Are you worth X dollars per hour? Should you be earning more?

Does your employer own your career or do you own it?

Do you only produce results when you are working or are you producing results around the clock?

Do you rest and relax or are your creating your empire of wealth?

Declaration: "I choose to get paid based on my results."

Wealth File #12:

Rich people think "both."
Poor people think "either/or."

Rich people believe "You can have your cake and eat it too." Middle class people believe, "Cake is too rich, so I'll only have a little piece." Poor people don't believe they deserve cake, so they order a doughnut, focus on the hole, and wonder why they have "nothing."

Everything is created for you. There is no limit to what you can receive on Earth.

Are you going to buy the blue suit or the black suit? Why not get both?!?

Do you like SUVs or sedans? Why not get both?!?

Will you invest in Seminar A or Seminar B? Why not invest in both?!?

Should I take Vacation 1 or Vacation 2? Go on both vacations!!

Should I get Book X or Book Y? Get both!!

Declaration: "I always think 'both'."
Declaration: "I get everything I need!"
Declaration: "There is no limit to my abundance!"
Declaration: "I own everything. Everything is for me!"

Wealth File #13:

Rich people focus on their net worth.

Poor people focus on their working income.

The true measure of wealth is net worth, not working income.

Where attention goes, energy flows and results show.

Do you have a cash flow of multiple investments or do you depend on a flat rate from your employer every week?

Do many streams of income do you have?

If you were to liquidate everything you have, what would be your net worth?

Are you purchasing more assets or liabilities?

Every dollar must contribute to building your net worth.

Will your purchase help you earn more money in the future?

Declaration: "I focus on building my net worth!"
Declaration: "My net worth is increasing every day!"

Declaration: "I am building my cash flow every day!"

Wealth File #14:

Rich people manage their money well.

Poor people mismanage their money well.

Until you show you can handle what you've got, you won't get any more!

The habit of managing your money is more important than the amount.

Either you control money, or it will control you.

Do you pay yourself first or do you pay everyone else?

Is there too much month at the end of the money or too much money at the end of the month?

"If you misuse it and confuse it, you lose it."-Daniel Ally

Declaration: "I am an excellent money manager."
Declaration: "I have full control of my money."

Wealth File #15:

Rich people have their money work hard for them.
Poor people work hard for their money.

Rich people see every dollar as a "seed" that can be planted to earn a hundred more dollars, which can then be replanted to earn a thousand more dollars.

You must not work for money, but let money work for you.

Do you wake up and see an increase in your bank account or is it always the same amount?

Do you earn money while you aren't working?

Declaration: "My money works hard for me and makes me more and more money."

Wealth File #16:

Rich people act in spite of fear.
Poor people let fear stop them.

Action is the "bridge" between the inner world and the outer world.

A true winner can "tame the cobra of fear" by controlling their emotions about money and working toward their goals.

If you are willing to do only what's easy, life will be hard. But if you are willing to do what's hard, life will be easy.

The only time you are actually growing is when you are uncomfortable.

In terms of happiness and success, training and managing your own mind is the most important skill you could ever own.

Declaration: "I act in spite of fear."
Declaration: "I act in spite of doubt."
Declaration: "I act in spite of worry."
Declaration: "I act in spite of inconvenience."
Declaration: "I act in spite of discomfort."
Declaration: "I act when I'm not in the mood."
Declaration: "I am a positive force in the world!"

"Don't let the fear of losing be greater than the excitement of winning." –Robert Kiyosaki

Wealth File #17:

Rich people constantly learn and grow.

Poor people think they already know.

Only the wisest people on Earth will seek the knowledge and skill to become smarter and better than yesterday.

The poor man will tell you everything he thinks you need to know about money. Do the exact opposite of what he says.

To get paid the best, you must be the best.

Declaration: "I am committed to constantly learning and growing."

"The mark of true wealth is determined by how much one can give away." – T. Harv Eker

-------------------------End of Wealth Files-------------------------

From these wealth principles, you may think this the breakthrough you need in your financial life. Hopefully, you understand these principles, and know that is only the beginning of wealth. There are many books that you can read on earning and increasing your income. I suggest reading "Think and Grow Rich" by Napoleon Hill and "Rich Dad, Poor Dad" by Robert Kiyosaki. Also read books on metaphysics. My favorite metaphysical book is by Charles Fillmore. It is called, "Prosperity." It is a hard book to find, but you will be blessed abundantly once you find it. These books will help you shape your mind. There are thousands to choose from. Be careful when choosing books regarding your wealth and its acquisition. Like religion, philosophy, and history books, some of them may be incorrect with their philosophies, so be very selective. Not all books will provide the absolute truth on true prosperity.

"Every master was once a disaster." – T. Harv Eker

Reading these books will only be the beginning of your wealth. You also need to do the work and get involved with applying the principles that you learn. There are other specific books that you will need to read about such as law, taxes, investments, accounting, etc. One needs to know the difference between assets and liabilities. The only way you can acquire money is by bringing value to the marketplace. Having strong selling and promotional skills are highly necessary to achieving financial freedom. You need to have many skills in order to become wealthy. You must also know how to manage and hire others. No one can become wealthy without hiring people to work with them. Create your own Master Mind (refer to Chapter 9).

The more valuable you are to the marketplace, the more you will be viewed as an asset and the harder it will be to replace you. For instance, someone who flips burgers at McDonald's can easily be replaced by anyone else. However, the CEO of Disney would need to be qualified with certain skills that a fast-food worker wouldn't necessarily possess. With money comes much responsibility. Many people cannot handle responsibility, nor do they want to. That is why they do not get money. It all starts with discipline. If you can have discipline, you can have as much money as you would like. With the proper mindset, you can earn money in a relatively easy fashion. It all begins with how you think about money.

I truly believe that any average person in the United States of America can accumulate a reasonable fortune in less than ten years. There is much to know about money and these books only cover the mindsets. There is still much more to learn. Put yourself in the right position and you can go anywhere in the financial world. The mints are making new money for your bank account. Go ahead, because the money is waiting for you. You are the Boss!

"Wealth is the ability to fully experience life."
–Henry David Thoreau

12

Power from Discipline

"Discipline is the bridge between thought and accomplishment."

-Jim Rohn

The topic of discipline and work ethic is rarely found. You can gain a lot of power by disciplining yourself and creating the proper work habits. Since we are all creatures of habits, we must know what habits we need to form to help us navigate through life. I know that when I try to look for ways to improve my effectiveness, there are only a few books and people who can help. This chapter will help you build or increase your momentum. We all learn by modeling. It is one of the most powerful forms of learning. In this chapter, I will add a few of my own habits. This chapter will cover how you can become more disciplined and what kind of work ethic you need to acquire to become a massive success and gain power in your lives.

Sleep

For years, experts have recommended eight hours of sleep per day. That usually works for most people. I have tried dozens of ways to sleep hack. Sleep-hacking is where you try to get less sleep to get more things done. I recommend that you do what works best for you. I know of some people who can be effective with four hours of sleep per day. Others may be restored with six hours per day. Many of my business acquaintances are sleeping about 7 to 7.5 hours per day. I usually sleep 6 to 6.5 hours per day and take a nap in the middle of the day. On Sundays I tend to sleep 8-9 hours. I am fully recharged by the time Monday comes.

I usually find it best to get in a rhythm of sleeping. It is best to wake up early. Many successful people wake up early. Let's take for example the former president, George H.W. Bush and his son George W. Bush. The first Bush would get up at 4 a.m., go running, be in the office by 6 a.m. and stay up until 2 a.m. He would take many naps during the day. The second Bush kept a similar schedule, going to the office by 6:45 a.m. and often holding meetings at that time. So did George W. Bush's cabinet. Colin Powell put in "perfectly appalling" hours, arriving at his office around 6 a.m., and not leaving until after 7 p.m. Condoleeza Rice woke up every day at 4:30 a.m. in order to get to the gym and read before work.

Benjamin Franklin, who is one of the most well-known forefathers in the United States of America is credited with the statement. "Early to bed and early to rise makes a man healthy, wealthy and wise." He planned his routine around waking up at 5 a.m. and asking himself, "What good shall I do this day?" He was definitely a man of achievement. That is probably why he is on your one-hundred dollar bill.

If you wake up late, perhaps 9 or 10 a.m., just start going to bed earlier. Set your mental clock back ten minutes each night before you sleep. For instance, if you sleep at 1 am, set it at 12:50 a.m., then 12:40 a.m. the next day. Do this until you are able to hit the desired time. A great deal can be done if you are able to get all of your tasks done when you first wake up.

You may be like me. I used to say to myself, "I am not a morning person. I am a night person." By using this declaration, you are teaching yourself to be a late person, but it doesn't mean that you are. You could be saying this just because you don't want to wake up early. Many people say it because other people say it as well. The worst thing you can do, in regards to sleeping, is to wake up inconsistently at different times. When I used to do this in my college days, it threw off my biological clock and I could not recover from my fatigue the rest of the day. This can be fixed by waking up at the same time every day.

Another good thing to do is to take naps. If you like to sleep late, but still want to wake up early, just do what they do in Spain. Take a siesta! This is simply a short 15-20 minute nap. It can be extended to 30-60 minutes or more, depending on your body. I didn't know how important this was until I went to Spain and quickly became accustomed to this tradition. They usually take a siesta right after their lunch in the afternoon. If you work during the day, you can take a nap after you get off of work. If you can get one of these in, it is a very special way to acquire the rejuvenation you need. Remember the '5 hour energy' commercials? No more 2 p.m. drowsy feelings anymore. With a short nap, it can instantly feel like a new day and a new you!

By doing this, you can stay up until 12 a.m. and still wake up at 6 a.m. Once again, it depends on who you are. If you can get two of these siestas in your day, you can cut down your sleep overnight. Beware that it will affect your REM sleep and dreaming capabilities. Sleeping has a proven relation to the way you think. It is said that the inventor, futurist, and engineer, Nikoli Tesla, claimed to not sleep over two hours. Instead, he would take many brief naps during the day. He believed that sleeping is a waste of time. You will find that there are so many ways to sleep. Research more about polyphasic sleep habits. There is more to sleeping than your conventional "8 hours" per night.

Reading

It takes a lot of discipline to read a book, but the benefits from doing it will be extraordinary. Literacy is instrumental in our lives and our development. When I first started to read, I read the Bible and it made me obsessive about reading. I began to read voraciously and devour every good book I could find relevant to my life, needs, and goals. I usually read one hundred books per year or more, but once again, it is my favorite hobby. I encourage your to read one book per month. This would mean that if you would read a three-hundred page book, you would have to read at a pace of ten pages a day for thirty days or one month. If you wanted to be very successful, you would read one book per week. A good reader can devour a three-hundred page book in a week if they put in the time and effort. If you really want to become good at reading, you will need many moments of silence and deep concentration.

It takes great diligence to choose a book, sit down, read and take good notes. Set yourself up for success by having a go-to place to read. If you want to be your best at reading get the book, "How to

Read a Book," by Mortimer Adler. It will redefine the way you read. He claims that most people read on an elementary level. You will grow tremendously by this piece of literature. Be warned that it is a very challenging book to read, but is well worth the time invested. Many claim that they do not have the time to read, but they are only cheating themselves on the promotions that could be gained in their lives. Reading provides a great advantage and helps you place a premium on your self-worth. Leaders are readers.

How to Approach Reading

Effective reading requires outlining, highlighting, referencing, note-taking, and thinking. Many times, people read books that are easy and skim through most of it. People do not read as much as they should. In order to be the best person you can be you must have a goal for reading. You must know exactly what you want out of a book and what kind of results. Most people do not have reading goals. They do not know what to read, how much to read, and when to read.

Setting timelines for your reading will help. Try to read the table of contents and know what kind of book you are reading. Is it informative, entertaining, practical, etc.? How many pages? What is the level of difficulty? How much time do you have to read it? All of these will help you set a realistic time to finish your book.

Hopefully, you will be able to finish earlier rather than later, unless you need more time to understand the concepts in the book you are reading. Reading takes up a lot of energy too. Many times, your mind may start wandering. Take a break if this happens to you. Depending on the person, you can take a reading break every 60-90 minutes if you are an experienced reader. Don't overdose on it and bore yourself with the reading material. When I first started reading, I would take a break every 15-30 minutes. Your endurance will build over time as you learn how to read.

What to Read and What Not to Read

It is also good to know what books to read and what books to stop reading. I remember one time I got into a five-hundred page book only to realize that this person did not have much depth in their writing. The book gave no illustrations and was very boring. The book was redundant and I quit reading it on page twenty. This led me to pick up another book, which turned out to be one of my favorite books. Be sure to use your reading time effectively. Read anything that can take you to the next level. Read only that which can transform your thinking.

Too often, people fall for 'mental candy' and read too many easy books. They never gain the substance that they could have and may only study one category of life. There are so many things to learn and so many authors who have contributed immensely to the library systems of the world. Everything you need to know in life can be found in all the books in the world. You must be selective in what books you want to read. Although most books will help you, some books can hurt you if you aren't careful enough. They can lead you astray if the author is persuasive and you adopt their fiction. If you feel that you are reading the wrong book, simply put it down. It may not be for you. There is a better book waiting for you.

You may want to avoid literature that may depreciate your health. Stay away from tabloids and gossip magazines. Beware of particular articles online, newspapers, and magazines that may slander something or someone. Do not waste your reading time on media that is irrelevant to your success. Do not read the comments that people leave on the internet either. People can get very nasty on the internet. Try not to read Facebook, Twitter, Linkedin, and other social media too frequently. There are many pieces of random literature in the world that will try to get your attention, but it does not deserve your time.

How Much to Read

I read about 15-20 hours per week. On a good week of growth, I can get up to 25-30 hours. I will get deep into the night if the book qualifies my attention. On Sundays, I try to read about 5-8 hours. The weekends are the majority of my reading time. Instead of going out to socialize on weekdays or weekends, I try to take those 4-5 hours to read. It would be best if you started by reading 15-30 minutes per day. After a few weeks or months, increase your reading time to 60-120 minutes per day. It is very common for a very influential person to read 3-4 hours per day. I always keep a book in my car, bedroom, bathroom, and more. This sets me up for reading as much as I could with all the time that I have. I suggest that you take a serious approach to reading and find time to get yourself into a position where you have the ability and willingness to read. Reading requires an appetite for knowledge and wisdom.

"Either write something worth reading or do something worth writing."-Benjamin Franklin

It is said that the Russian dictator, Josef Stalin read 400 pages per day. I tried to match that, but I can only do 100-150 pages on the best days. Usually I read about 40-60 pages per day. The best that I have done in one day was 315 pages, but I read for 16 hours straight on a snowy day. It also depends on the type of book in which I am reading. I study diligently when I am reading. I do not settle for easy books. Try to work your way up to as many pages as you could. Also, it is helpful to record your thoughts as you are reading on a sheet a paper. This will help you to relate and assimilate the concepts that leap across your mind. You will retain much more when you write down your thoughts. This should substantially help you.

Audio Books

Audio books are a joy to listen to, but I do not consider it reading. I do not get to take the notes that I want and usually do not revisit the audio book after I hear it the first time. They are good to put into your CD player while you are driving or in your iPod when you are working out, sitting in the airport, or walking somewhere. You can even sit down and listen to an audio book. Many of the books you read can be found on audio books. Zig Ziglar calls it

"Automobile University," because it can help you develop immeasurably. I usually get through 2 or more per month, or 20-30 per year. They are great learning tools. For me, it's better than music and talk shows.

Most people take an hour per day to commute in their vehicles. In a given year, can get anywhere from 300-1000 hours of audio books into your incredible minds. Most public libraries have good audio books that you can find and order for free. It is a big difference maker and a good alternative to listening to music or talk shows. I will have many of them that you will be able to purchase in the future.

Memory

Remembering things is very important. People cheat their memories all the time. Have you ever heard someone say "Don't trust your memory?", "I always forget?", "I can never remember peoples' names?" I used to fall in this category and cheat myself in the same way as well. Now, I can remember the names of 20-25 people when I meet them in a room. When I started reading Tony Buzan's books, it exposed me to a whole new world of memorizing and retaining what you know. Memory will help us grow tremendously once you know how to use it. People often stop learning because they feel that they do not have the capacity to remember anything. Mnemonics can change the way you feel about memory.

"Memory is the diary that we all carry about with us."-Oscar Wilde

Mnemonics will help you to coordinate certain traits about a person, place, or thing to help you memorize something in particular. Since humans think in pictures, we can remember people from their hairstyles, noses, or cars. But is this enough? What if we can consider everything about a person by assiduously studying them and take it to a whole new level by remembering them thoroughly? What if you can remember the names of peoples' kids, the cars they drive, their personal stories, their dogs, and everything else?

I learned that memorizing anything is possible when I was taught by studying Tony Buzan's memory tactics. I will not go into any details; I just want you to know that the tools are available for you to start memorizing more. Go out and get some of his books. You can build your short-term and long term memories this way. You can remember numbers, details, and various things. Our minds are very powerful and we should always remember that. Building your memory could help you grow in many areas of your life if you develop it. There are some people who are born with the capability to remember information, but most of the people, including you, can learn many of the memory tricks available to you. You are the Boss!

Languages

Becoming a polyglot is something that we can all do. We can learn foreign languages to be able to connect with people of different cultures. You should be able to be competent in your native language before you try to pursue others. If English is your main language, work on it constantly. Always read the dictionary and thesaurus while pronouncing words out loud. Always practice it when you are alone and with people. Never get lazy in your usage of language. It is good to know the derivation of words and certain foreign phrases and proverbs of various cultures. Words are powerful and they are the tools by which we leave impressions on our minds and those of others.

Language shapes our world. If we do not understand it, we will not have the power to do what we must in this world. Everyone should know how to communicate effectively. However, this is not the case and it is actually improbable to find someone who is perfect with their language. Once you develop a powerful foundation for language, no one can control you, because you can express the exact meaning of anything that you are trying to say. It is always to know a few phrases in different languages. Rosetta Stone is a very good way to learn different languages. There are also courses that you can take or videos that are online that you can watch.

Gold Calls

Operating the phone and email is an important thing to do if you want to gain success. The phone and email is a valuable and easy way to earn money once you learn the skills required of its usage. If I had not used the phone or email properly, I would have missed out on many opportunities. Sometimes we think that we should or should not reach out to a person. Do it anyways. Stop reasoning with yourself and take action. It is a strange concept to think that there is another person at the end of the phone line or email that is going to curse us out or reject us.

Actually, the opposite is true. Most people you want to call will be happy to talk to you once you make the phone call or send them an email. Sometimes we think too deeply about making the phone call or sending an email. I call them 'gold calls' because they sound better and serves more people than 'cold calls.' The phone will change you once you understand how it works. Also, be sure to use an updates Smartphone. It is worth the price you pay and it will give you access to the world.

If your work requires you to make 'gold calls' (cold calls), be sure not to treat people like a number. Instead, treat them like a person. Remember, while quality and quantity are both important, the quality of your calls will help you more. Even though it may be a 'numbers game' in your business and you want to reach quotas, people have the need to feel important. They do not feel important if you treat them like a number. Do not overload yourself with too many phone calls at once. Be sure to switch up your voice. Voice control is very important when making the 'gold call.' You do not want to sound artificial or intimidate anyone. Never sound rushed or anxious. People will know if you have the 'next' mentality. They know when you are speeding through your list to get to the next call.

A few years ago, a woman was making her rounds of follow up calls. When she called me, we spoke briefly about the opportunity she wanted to present to me. It was about 1 minute into the conversation that I said, 'thank you,' then she abruptly hung up the phone. I was appalled, because I had no intention of hanging up when I said 'thank you,' but I knew she wasn't happy with her job by the tone and rashness of her voice. Instantly, I realized that she had a 'next' mentality and quickly forgave her. Phone calls do not end on 'thank you,' they end on 'goodbye.' Set yourself up with post-it notes to remind yourself to keep a pace when making 'gold calls.' You will want to take copious notes and get organized for each call. Prepare the right questions for the right people for the right time.

Set a goal for when you want to make calls and how many calls or appointments you want. Be as personable as you can be. Always be smiling when dialing. Never make 'gold calls' when you are angry or upset. Take frequent breaks and rejuvenate yourself with a beverage. Do not become undisciplined by eating around your desk or texting while making 'gold calls.' Always remember your purpose for making the call. If you forget your purpose, people will forget you. If you have a difficult time getting started, talk to yourself and remind yourself why you are doing what you are doing. Walk around the room or outside if you have to. Pick up the phone and make the calls. You already know how much your calls will pay off when the check comes.

What about someone who wants to use the phone for family purposes and not business? A woman I met had to ask for forgiveness from her father. She could not move on in life because there was a disaster that kept playing in her mind. She thought that she had done the worse thing possible by not being in contact with him. I told her that she would be benefited if she would simply call her father after fifteen years to apologize for her rebellion. As she called, I stood and listened. Within the first minute, both people broke down in tears because the phone call had always needed to be made. There was a buildup of emotion that overflowed like a raging river. It wasn't even because of what she said, but the fact that she made the call. Do you need to make this kind of phone call?

What if she never made the call? There would have never been peace or unity made in the family. Unfortunately, this happens frequently. People neglect making important phone calls to friends and families because of the 'voices in their head.' Never let it happen to you. Make the family call if needed. It doesn't matter who is right or wrong. Be the bigger person and make the call. The phone is waiting.

Do you need to use the phone or email to find work? Most of the jobs I had gotten were a phone call or email away. All I needed to do is make a call or two. Sometimes I would be hesitant to make a phone call or send an email, and so I began to say to myself, "I have everything to gain by making this phone call." What good would it be if you didn't make the phone call or send an email? By learning proper techniques of sending emails and using the phone correctly, you can impress people with your communication. There are many books on the subject of phone and email skills.

One of my colleagues taught me a very important tip that I want to share with you. She called it '5 by 10.' This is where you make your 5 most important phone calls by 10 a.m. Why? Most busy people handle phone calls and emails early on and you can reach them in that moment, they will be ready for you. Not only this, they will detect that you are more serious rather than you calling at 2 p.m. or 5 p.m. in the day. It makes a dramatic difference when you make the phone calls before 10 a.m., especially if you need to get to decision-makers and other people who are hard to reach. If you do it after 10 a.m., those are also the times that people are thinking about their next meal or their families. Plus, you won't have to stare at the phone all day and think about when you will make the call. It is one of the best phone tips that I have ever heard. Your phone is one of your best business tools.

With emailing, be sure to learn how to set up your emails the correct way. Add your name, phone number, and business address (if applicable). Never junk up your email with all the additional information that a particular person does not need. Sometimes, people try to get fancy with their emails by using words they don't know or adding long quotes, jokes, or stories. Never do this. You do not want to come off as someone you are not. Do not send attachments related to your business when you do not need to. Always keep emails simple. Add a little jazz if you could, but never overwhelm anyone.

It is always good to follow up with people. After I do business with a client, I always try to give them a phone call or email. You can also use an email to summarize a meeting or phone call. Do not substitute emails with text messages. Keep it professional by staying in contact and letting them know that you still exist. Never sell over the phone or email (unless that is your particular business requires it.) Use the phone and email to set appointments and give information. It is an excellent way to earn repeat business.

Remember that email and cell phone usage is for your benefit, not merely to serve everyone else agenda. Do not be a slave to inbound communication irrelevant to your success. Unsubscribe to people's list if it has nothing to do with your success. Keep separate emails for personal and business use. You may have more than two email addresses. Create folders for necessary categories and delete emails regularly. Strive to check emails 3-6 times per day or less. Many people check emails every hour. They are constantly at the will of other peoples' agenda. This leaves them in a reactive rather than proactive state of mind. *End of email and phone advice.*

To add an extra-special touch in your relationships, send a personal letter or a thank-you card. It will blow people away. They will appreciate you more than ever. Have you ever gotten a thank-you card before? If you have, you know the kind of love it exhibits. It shows that you put in extra time and care to send one out to a particular person. A thank-you card is one the best inexpensive gifts that can be given. It will take you to higher places. There is no one who will turn one down. In fact, many will keep them as long as possible. No one ever forgets a thank-you card, especially when it comes at the right time. People love individual attention. Nancy Reagan sent many thank-you cards. That is probably one of the ways Ronald Reagan became president. Find as many creative ways to stay in touch with people. Send them anything valuable. The secret of living is giving.

Surrounding Yourself with the Right People

Never forget that you are directly influenced with the people in your environment. It is said that you are the sum total of the five people your hang around the most. You start to develop the same habits, think alike, and partake in the same activities as they do. As I mentioned earlier in the book, my mother used to tell me, "I know who you are by judging who your friends are." It took me a long time to understand that, but once I did, I was never the same again.

Most people are raised in an environment that cannot assist them with becoming what they were created to be. Many people around your may have the right intentions, but do not always provide the right directions. During your lifetime, thousands of people will give you advice. Most of them will not be good for your. You must be able to discern whether or not their advice will help you with your dream.

"Your dream is not for sale" – Craig Valentine

When I graduated college, I thought it would have been a decent job to sell luxury vehicles. My boss at the time talked about how I would receive good pay, a luxury car to drive, my own office, business cards, clientele, and everything a luxury car salesperson would need to succeed in that particular business. All of this was good until I started to realize what kind of people I was working with. As I began to interview my co-workers, they told me about their failures in particular careers and how they ended up selling luxury vehicles. None of them wanted to be there and they were living a regretful life.

One man talked about how the mortgage business had robbed him, alongside a plethora of excuses. Another man told me how managing a home improvement store required the leadership he didn't think he possessed. Another woman was fired from her waitressing job. Someone else told me that they did not get their dream job because they could not pass an examination that the job required. I started to realize that the people that I was surrounded with let their circumstances tell them where they were going. I found that their negative mindsets started to have a subtle effect on me. Even though the job seemed good at the time, it wasn't worth being there because of the people I was working with.

They became resentful toward me because I did not partake in their mundane discussions about sports, music, news, and pop culture. They were envious because I was focused on becoming the best I could be on the job. A woman who I worked with set me up for failure when I was delivering a vehicle on the second week. She misplaced a crucial folder that I needed to give my clients. I had sold more vehicles than all five of them combined that week.

Even though I could have done exceptionally working at the dealership, it would be bloodshed if I kept working there. It was not exactly what the sales manager told me it would be. I sensed this early on when I first interviewed for the job, but I ignored the instinct. Anyone who would not conform to the status quo would be crucified. I was surrounded by very envious and jealous people who did not like what I came to do. They were sending very obvious hints. I knew I had to get out quickly before it was too late.

There was too much hostility going on in the workplace. Some were indirect and others were more direct. I did not need the excessive drama. If I didn't make the move, you would not be reading this book right now. That day, I made a promise to myself that very day that I would never put myself in situations (or jobs) where I could not grow, despite how well I got paid or how reputable the company was. My whole world changed when I took the leap of faith to start my own business.

"All our dreams can come true, if we have the courage to pursue them." - Walt Disney

You too can make a decision today to be around the right people who can help you achieve your dreams. First, you need to know where you want to go. Second, you need to know who can help you get there. There are many vehicles that can take you to the right destination. For me, the luxury dealership wasn't the destination, but the creation of my business was. Find a place where you fit and go there. You will begin to develop in ways in which you could have never imagined. Here are some excuses people make. Run as far as you can when you hear them uttered. I got some of these from David Schwartz's book, "The Magic of Thinking Big." I added two extra excuses and put my own twist to them.

Six Excuses People Make:

1. **Health-** Many people will talk about how their health prohibits them from growing. They talk about how asthma prevents them from jogging or how diabetes prevents them from traveling. People will always come up with health excuses. Some of them will not even be verbalized. Sometimes you can look at someone and you can physically see that they are overweight and are defeated by it. Some people skip major life-altering events because they say they had the flu, slight headache, or any other perceived illnesses. They have a bruised bone or an ankle injury and that is all your will ever hear from them. You will probably hear people discuss their sickness in the marketplace. Some will talk about how cancer stopped them from living their dreams.

    Others may say that they are disabled from a job and they settled for worker's compensation. Then there are others who have gotten laid-off at a corporation and get on the 99-week unemployment program.

    There are some who claim to not have the energy like "other people do." They blame their eyesight or the deafness in one ear. They say that they are insomniacs and that is the reason why they are always late to their jobs. People who claim they have health conditions go around telling everyone why they can't do it and they think people really believe them. They sometimes diagnose themselves with sicknesses that they do not even have. They are hypochondriacs, which mean they excessively create worries for their health, which is usually their detriment.

2. **Age**- They say “I am too old to try that.” Or “I am not the way I used to be when I was 30.” They talk about how they are way past their prime. Many will say that they have many ‘senior moments’ or are ‘getting old.’ They talk about how the job they applied for had discriminated against them because they were too old. These people sell themselves short all their lives because they listen to other people complain about their age, so they do it too. Many people fail to change their careers when they know they should. They think that it is too late to get into a different line of work, even if they are in their thirties. They live lives of quiet desperation and they end up dying with major frustrations with deep feelings of incompleteness, resentment, bitterness, and nonfulfillment.

Some will say that they are too old to go back to school or get specialized training. I have met many elderly people who “knew it all.” They are completely unteachable. These people always tell me, “I wish I were as young as you, I would....” Most of the people who use the age excuse have nothing to offer you and will do anything to tell you why their age has stopped them from becoming who they could have been.

Elderly people will not take certain jobs because of their pride. They believe they deserve better treatment since they had their 'glory days' in the past. The marketplace doesn't reward you for your past, only for your present state of mind. There is no way around this. Any person at any age can start all over again. All they need to do is acknowledge that they must start again.

There are also people who limit themselves by thinking that they are too young. A man in his teens may be asked to be a manager at a retail or restaurant environment, but may not believe in himself because of his inexperience. From experience, I have been asked to be promoted many times, but I often thought that I was too young to take the job. I didn't think I was worthy and thought I would be hated. I thought the job paid too much. These excuses of age work well for many people because no one can control their actual age.

3. **Luck-** Some say that they are not the right skin color. They believe that they were born to the wrong parents. They blame other people for their disposition and cannot blame anyone by themselves. They say things like "it takes too much time" or "I had to watch my mother die for five years as I took care of her. I had no choice." They create irrefutable excuses. They know that their reason is the right reason to not be able to do it.

They may think that they do not have the physical appearance. They say they aren't tall enough and "I couldn't be a cop, I am only 5' 8" or "most good quarterbacks in the NFL are 6'2" or models have to be tall and thin to make it in the fashion business. They say, "I couldn't get into the fashion industry because my cheekbones are too high" or "my dimples are too deep." They say, "My hair is too curly." These people have the most excuses. These people usually think they can win the lottery, and then when other people win it, they attribute the winner as being 'lucky.' My favorite excuse is "I don't have a car, so I couldn't get to work to earn money to buy one." Or "I couldn't go to school because I had kids early." They have one million excuses and you have heard most of them. They think successful people cheat, lie, and steal to get to their position in life. Luck is the determining factor for success to them. Stay away from these people or they will start to blame you too.

4. **Weather** -Every day you will hear people complaining about the weather. This is another common excuse because no one has control over it. People will not attend events because there is too much snow. Others will complain about how the rain stopped their parade. Schools will shut down if it is too cold. Children can't get their parents to take them to amusement parks because it's too windy. People will not devote themselves to learning if the weather is too nice. They have to go outside and 'play.' They say, "It's too nice to stay

inside today." Conversely, others say that they will get to a certain project when the weather gets better. Some will even pray that the weather is poor so that they will not have to go to where they do not want to go. I never saw a mailman complaining about the weather (except when he's making small talk). When you have a purpose and a job to do, the weather will rarely be able to stop you from doing it. I once drove 5 hours in thick snow to give an unpaid speech to 3 people. My audience got the message.

"An indomitable temperament will overcome the most severe weather." -Daniel Ally

5. **Money**-"I can't make it to the conference because it cost too much." It actually costs more to not get there. If I did not fork up all of my money to go to the seminars I knew I needed to attend, I would not be who I am today. Many people will fall short and say that they cannot join because the "fees are too high." They also say, "It costs too much" and "I can't afford it." Many will skip college because they are overwhelmed with their tuition costs. People fail to make changes in their lives because of money problems.

"Money is a tool used to separate minds." -Shivanee Patel

Many people will not invest in themselves because they think that the money is too much. They say, "If I had the kind of money he had, I would invest in real estate." They also say that they would give more if they had more money to give. We live in a world where money is not the actual problem, but motive is. If your motives are right, the money will always be there. Money is always available for anything that your heart desires. They never stop making it, unless the world came to an end. Now you know why they call it an 'end'!

6. **Intelligence**-They say that "only if I had a degree, license or certificate, I would do it." People limit themselves substantially because they think they need credentials. You don't need credentials to make a substantial contribute. We all have intelligence and genius in different ways. Some have more than others. How can a natural-born painter look at a businessman and say "If I had his intelligence, I would…"? It doesn't make any sense to say that you are not good enough because you are not smart enough or have the right credentials. Never demote yourself by thinking that you aren't good enough. There are some people who seemed qualified in this world who cannot do the job at all. There are others with no qualifications that can create quality work. Credentials can help, but it doesn't determine your intelligence and will not limit you. When you limit yourself in any way, other people will limit you. If you are unlimited in your thinking, people will flock to you. You don't always

need a title, position, degree, certificate, and license. If you are the best at what you do, nothing can stop you.

"An investment in knowledge pays the best interest."
-Benjamin Franklin

It's always better to know more than you need to know. Jim Rohn said, "The book you don't read won't help you." The skill you don't have will hurt you, especially if you need it. It is better to find out what you do not know and learn it. Ignorance is not bliss, it's an atrocity. The lack of knowledge causes major insecurity for many people. Real education is using everything that you know, not merely the accumulation of facts. Many people know many things, but few know what to actually do about it. This is called wisdom, and wisdom makes the difference. Wisdom is knowing what to do with your natural abilities and current resources. My life philosophy is, "You have to take what you get in life to get what you want out of life."

There are many opportunities to learn and gain wisdom. Did you ever notice that everyone wants a front row seat at places of entertainment, but they all gather to the back when it comes to church and education? The truth is that you can always learn and you should constantly be endeavoring yourself to learning new skills and rebuilding your mind. Sit in the front when it comes to learning. There is always a lesson to learn.

------------------------------*End of Excuses*-----------------------------

I am not saying that none of these excuses are legitimate reasons why a person cannot succeed. All I am saying is that when people start to discuss these things, you will learn that they are not committed to being the best. When people resort to these acts of deception, they hurt themselves and other people as well. Once you understand that people come with these excuses, you will be able to detect what kind of people you are dealing with.

Be prepared to be surprised with what you find. Search for people who are positive and never make excuses. Find people who will help you nourish your dreams. If you are passionate and really want to do something, your mind will change to "it is not who is going to let me do it, but who is going to stop me from doing it." This momentous mindset will take you places. An old preacher once said, "If you set yourself on fire, people will come to watch you burn!" It is time to get the fire of your dream started!!

Thinking and Reflecting with Quiet Time

We need time for thinking and reflection. Quiet time is one of the finest ways to gain power, authority, and discipline. If we are around people for more than eight hours at a time, things can become overwhelming and we are not as effective. You need a thinking chair or an area where we can dedicate your time to think. Your car, bed, and shower are great places to think because you are alone. Nevertheless, I highly recommend a designated area where you can think about your strategies and plan your actions. Usually, you will find that in the car, bed, or shower, you are unable to write down your thoughts without hassle. You are more likely to capture your ideas on paper when you have a special area in which you can think. Get away from all of the commotion to get to your deepest thoughts.

"Think in the morning, act in the noon, read in the evening, and sleep at night." - William Blake

Without the proper thinking and reflecting time in a quiet area, you lose the opportunity to know yourself as much as you could. You are less likely to plan and produce as much as you could because you did not think out all of the options you really have in your life. Most people fail because they do not use the gift that the Creator gave them, and that gift is the ability to think. Thinking must be done deliberately, but most people do it accidentally. When you have the time to think, you are more able to discern and capitalize on better opportunities in your life. You will be able to know exactly what you want. You can reflect on your day to see what must be improved. You can create strategies on how to approach a person and various situations. With thinking time, you can stretch your imagination and learn more about the world you live in and the people you are surrounded by.

"If everyone is thinking alike, then somebody isn't thinking."

- George Patton

Most people do not allocate thinking time because they are afraid of their thoughts. Thinking is the most challenging thing to do because your mind must be trained to do it. If you make your mind your slave, you will have dominion over it and you can tell it what to do, instead of it telling you what to do. Many people are conquered by their own thoughts and do not know how to intelligently direct their minds into the right kind of thinking. Distractions also keep us from thinking the right thoughts. You have everything it takes to control your thoughts evade distractions.

It may feel strange when you do this at first, but your mind will reveal to you things in which you never thought you could think of. Solutions will start to come to you as soon as you utilize your thoughts. When you begin to think in an organized fashion, your mind eliminates trivial things and re-create new priorities that you must pursue. It will reveal to you how you can focus on the major things in life, rather than the minor things in life. A walk in the park with the serene nature is a peaceful way to gain access to your thoughts. Brainstorming alone can also help your thoughts.

The best way to think is to sit down at a desk and think with a pen and paper. Joyce Meyer, the evangelist, said "A #2 pencil and a dream can take you anywhere." Your vision will begin to develop and the call to excellence will be well within your grasp. As soon you begin to think, you will become more proactive, rather than reactive. Proactive is when you are able to anticipate circumstances that come to you. Reactive is when circumstances approach you and you do not know what to do. Sometimes things may be out of our control, which happens frequently.

Most of the times, we can have control over our mind and actions in our lives. Naturally, a crisis will happen in your life every 1-3 months. A crisis can become small once you acknowledge this. If you start to take time for serious thoughts, you can become far bigger than your problems. Dominating your mind begins by dominating your thoughts. Your mind is where all of your great ideas are born.

Exercise

Exercise is vitally important to anyone who wants to be successful. I have seen overweight and out-of-shape people who have been successful. In order to be well-rounded (No pun intended), one must constantly monitor their physical condition. Exercise must be taken very seriously. If you exercise 20-60 minutes per day 3-6 times per week, you should be good. Allow yourself 5-10 hours per week and take care of your physical body.

My exercise regimen is 1-2 heavy lifting sessions and I run 10-20 miles per week, which are 4-6 running sessions every week. Seldom do I play basketball. When I lift weights sometimes I lift socially with friends or by myself, depending on my current need or schedule. I use a monitor all of my exercises Never get into a rut while exercises. If you get bored or don't find an exercise working for you, switch it up to confuse your muscles and stimulate your mind. Muscle confusion and mental stimulation is very good for your body. Lifting is very good for confidence, appearance, and physical strength. You need all of these to be the best you can be.

I stretch every morning, day, and night. Flexibility and coordination is very important for your body. I run on the treadmill, on the track, in the neighborhood, or on the beach if I can find one. Running helps me think and dream big. My best ideas come while I am running. Try to wear comfortable shoes when running. Insert soles for your feet when necessary. Find the best attire to go running and wear light and breathable material. If I run in the cold, I dress very warmly. Always leave room for sweat. Running is my best and favorite exercise. It keeps the weight off and I can think and breathe easier.

I also play basketball because I like to jump around and socialize once in a while. I try to limit it because it is time consuming and I am very susceptible to injury when I play, especially when there in pressure in the game. Basketball helps me relieve my mind from stress. I never play basketball if I have deadlines to meet and a desk full of work to do. I get into a different dimension when I play basketball. I really do have passion for the game, but not enough to go to the NBA. The basketball reaches my hands about once a month and friends are glad to meet me on the court. My game is beautiful and intelligently played. It is an excellent chance for me to transfer my leadership and time-management skills in the game. It is a good game if you understand it. To relieve some stress in your life, find a game or hobby you love and get involved.

Hobbies can be used for exercise. Make sure you do something vigorous. As much as I love chess, it is not a physical exercise, but it is great from mental awareness. If you are a cheerleader or former cheerleader, I am one who supports cheerleading as a sport. Find something that fits your style of living. Some people like to swim, go rock-climbing, jump on the trampoline (very good exercise), do boxing or other fighting, yoga, Zumba, biking, and various exercises. There is something out there for you that I may not have listed. Go ahead and try as many as you like.

Exercising relieves you of your daily stresses and is best for your health. It enhances your life and allows you to be more confident in your skin. It also gives more endurance and keeps your awake during the day. When you do, your mind will become sharper, your focus will increase, and you will produce more results. You will live longer and be healthier. You will become more creative than ever before!

Diet

There is no perfect diet for everyone. People require different foods for religious and regional purposes. Certain foods will be found in certain places. I recommend that you find the right diet for yourself. It is better to eat less food more frequently, rather than a lot of food in a lump sum. In America, we see many people who overeat. People resort to fast-food restaurants at an all-time high, people are eating more secretly than ever. On the contrary, there are many diets being created and many of them exist for the sole purpose of earning money. The best diet is the one that is non-excessive. The less food you eat, the less likely you will be obese. The thought that I like to live by in regards to anything, especially eating is "everything in moderation, nothing in excess".

I used to be a connoisseur of greasy foods, and then I realized that it showed up in my physical appearance. I did not have the same energy as I did when I didn't eat fried food, and I could wake up out of bed even easier. It also appeared on my face and my skin. All of a sudden, I started to intake less greasy food, and I have lost forty pounds in the process. I went from 225 pounds on a 6 foot frame to 185 pounds.

The best diet is the vegetarian diet. I am not a vegetarian, but I commend vegetarians a lot because it is a challenging diet to be on, especially when you go out to eat. If you are vegetarian, good job! Although I am not a vegetarian, I have greatly reduced all of my meat consumption. I do not think I will become a vegetarian, but I also do not think that I will also gulp down a twenty ounce steak either. I also realized that a few ounces of lean meat will do, rather than a pound of a very fatty meat. If you can eat a pound of meat a week as an omnivore, you would be doing very well.

There are a lot of foods with cholesterol and high fats. Make sure you read your labels and get the proper ingredients that you need. Never be deficient in any substance necessary for a proper nutrition. Try to buy organic food as much as you can. Stay away from boxed and canned food. Avoid monosodium glutamate (MSG) and false sugars. There are many foods that have artificial ingredient that will destroy your biology if you are aware of it. Staying organic is the best way to go.

Avoid alcohol, tobacco, marijuana, painkillers or any other drugs. If you use any of these, you should know you need to quit. Sometimes it is difficult to change, but slow and steady will do it. Reduce steadily if you can. I have done all of these and I know for sure that you can be more happy without it. I never thought that I could stop until I started reading the Bible. All of a sudden, I eradicated all of the toxins that entered my body. These toxins destroy your taste buds and physical appearance. It also makes you smell badly. It messes up your mind and body. You may eat less food or more food depending on what drug you take, but this is the worse way to get on a diet. The long-term consequences will always catch up with you. No matter what anyone thinks, using these substances is absolutely wrong and noxious to your health. I sternly believe it from personal experience. Abstain from these substances as much as you can, even if you hate reading this paragraph.

Your body is your palace, and it is the only place you have to live! If you take care of it, it will take care of you. The best thing that you can do for yourself is drink plenty of water. Water helps your body cleanse itself. Science claims 64 fluid ounces, or eight cups per day is good, but I recommend drinking more. I normally consume one-hundred fluid ounces per day or more. Always drink water when you wake up and before you sleep. It will give you more energy. Drink in the summer as much as you would in the winter. Some people think that you sweat more in the summer, and you need more water because of it, but you use a lot of energy trying to stay warm in the winter too.

Drink plenty of water all the time. Drink more when you exercise or take up any physical activities. Always have a glass by your side when you are in your study, in your car, at work, and near your bed. Stay clear from any sodas and sweet beverages. Juices are good, as long as they are all natural and from fruits. You can also make smoothies made from real fruit. This is an excellent substitute for ice cream. A good alternative for chips are nuts and dried fruit. A poor diet can easily be replaced by a healthier one.

Never leave your beverage or food alone, someone may poison you. Even if you think they are your friends, watch out. What I am saying can happen to you, whether you are famous or not! We are all susceptible to this. Always watch your food and drinks. Be sure you know how it is being prepared. This may sound like a joke, but there are people out there who have done things like this. Don't be suspicious or let people know that you know this, just be calm about it. If you don't trust your food, kindly reject it.

Always make good decisions while eating. The choices you make today can help you tomorrow. You can live many years longer. Many people suffer because they choose to eat indiscriminately. We can make healthy choices every day. We can live healthily for one-hundred years or we can succumb to temporary pleasures of food all our lives and end life early. Death is certain, but so is life and our food is the fuel that can make it more pleasant. Sometimes it is difficult to maintain a healthy diet, especially as you travel, but learning how to adapt and choosing the right foods can take you a long way. Sometimes you can use good food to reward yourself. Find a system that works for you.

When going to a banquet, don't eat all the food. Instead, eat something light right before you come. Do not overdose on dessert of any kinds. Try to eat as much home cooked food as you can. Eat right until you feel that you will be full. You should eat no more than the size of your clenched fist. The better choices you make now, the better your body will serve you later. There are many books that you can find on diets and recipes that can help you eat better. There are many experts on the culinary field. Whatever you do, enjoy what you eat, but take it seriously. Do not live to eat, but eat to live. And remember, "Everything in moderation, nothing in excess." The choice is in your hands (pun intended). You are the Boss! Now eat like the Boss!

Sex and Romance

Sex and romance can be either the most beautiful or most detrimental act between human beings. When sex is used correctly, it can foster growth and harmony among two people. If sex is not used correctly, people can destroy their souls for misusing it. Many use it for pleasure only. Today, there is less love in sex mass media is completely redefining its sacred meaning. What many of us are exposed to is the complete opposite of what sex and romance actually represents.

Because of the simple fact that 'sex sells,' a lot of people are buying it. Behind closed doors, millions of Americans struggle with pornography. People seek instant gratification. The thoughts are becoming "my sexual needs require some kind of outlet," rather than, "I want and choose to have sexual relations with one particular person that I love." Meeting an unmarried adult who is a virgin is becoming rarer as time moves along. People are turning more to the same-sex relationships because they are confused about what sex represents.

This misconduct hurts the people who do it, and more importantly, the observing children who are involved. There are many single-parent households because of unplanned children. Sex has become a thoughtless and sometimes selfish act. People have less shame in their sexual debauchery. People are addicted to these licentious acts of sex. There are many sex stores, night clubs, sexual explicit websites, and strip clubs in the country that supports this fact. Advertisements and trigger words are becoming more common. The other day, I saw a billboard that advertised a steak dinner at a strip club. Another time, a man walked up to me and after five minutes of conversation, he told me about how much money he is making with his banner ads on the internet that leads to dating and sex sites. He had no idea that what he was supporting was completely wrong. In the Bible, it clearly states that the sex sin is the worst kind of transgression.

"Run from sexual sin! No other sin clearly affects the body as this one does. For sexual immorality is a sin against your own body."

-1 Corinthians 6:18 (New Living Translation)

Adultery and prostitution is at an all-time high. Men and women are looking for outlets to feel appreciated and use sex as the means to achieve attention, which they cannot obtain from their spouses. Some keep separate cell phones to maintain their adulterous relationships. Everywhere you go in American cities, you see married women with cleavage and seductive pants. There are men who remove their rings to freely flirt with others. Friends are even supporting this and acting like lookouts. Seduction has become customary and expected as people flatter each other into salacious acts. They deceive their innocent spouse who is waiting for their 'love' to come home and attend family matters while they act like they are 'golfing' or 'shopping.'

Flirting and flattery has trapped many married people into adultery. The craziest thing is that they never think that they will get caught! They go home and expect to live their normal life. They don't realize that the same energy that they take to escape the relationship can be used directly to mend it. Don't let me get preachy here.

What do we do about this? When children witness this, they lose their identity. They are modeling their parents (lack of parents) behaviors. Children can only receive unconditional love with loving and fully-functioning parents who communicate effectively. Children start to question things when they find out that there are different family structures (homosexual families). The misusage of sex and romance is unjustifiably selfish and highly immoral behavior. It is an abomination to God and the human race. Sex and romantic relationships must maintain its godly existence to be successful.

What about the good things that sex can do? The power behind a good loving couple and a family can be a tremendous asset. When a man and woman are together and respect each other's sexual needs, harmony and euphoria can take place. The proper usage of sex can create an unstoppable family. It can become heaven on Earth.

Historians often forget that Abraham Lincoln had a woman who he deeply loved named Anne Rutledge. Lincoln was a mediocre lawyer who failed at almost everything in his early days. When Anne Rutledge contracted typhoid at the age of 22, her death had cost Lincoln much sorrow. This drove Lincoln's emotions to succeed. He continued to live his life as though Anne Rutledge was still living. Even Shakespeare said that he would be nothing without Anne Hathaway, who was his beloved wife. There are thousands of examples of couples who used sex and romance in their path to power.

Most men would not be living without the romance of their wives. I know for me personally, life would be useless without a woman who loves me. Lincoln also said, "All that I am, and all that I ever hope to be I owe to my mother." Men live for women, and vice-versa. Love doesn't only have to be between husbands and wives. It can also be among parents, siblings, children, and intimate friends and relatives. I am a 'Momma's boy' and I love to please my mother, which is a hard thing to do. Most successful men have a strong mother and/or father that they become successful for. Without Barack Obama's mother's and grandmother's love, he would not have had the courage to become president of the United States. Men are driven by women, and vice versa.

If you look into the Bible, Adam and Eve lived for each other. In the Scriptures, it states that Eve was to be Adam's helper. The Bible shows the perfect way a man and woman should relation as they live their lives. When reading the Bible, be sure to read the entire book. If you read it with an open mind, you can learn all you need to know. My favorite part about the role of a wife is in Proverbs 31:10. If a woman can do what it states in that passage, she will be a 'perfect wife.' The love of a woman is supernatural.

All great men are influenced by a woman! Observe that whenever a man and woman pool their emotions together, there is a spirit of harmony, and the attainment of a definite end, and they become almost invincible against all forms of discouragement and temporary defeat. The proper use of sex and romance can multiply the creativity of a couple and take them to the highest level of thinking. When you think below the belt too often, your mind gets distracted from your true goals.

The emotion of sex will not be denied some form of expression! It resembles a river in that it can be dammed up and its powers diverted into whatever forms of action one desires, but it cannot be shut off from expression. If it is not released under controlled conditions, like a dam with overflowing water, it will break out by the sheer force of its own inherent power, in ways that can be very destructive. This is why people commit to sexual sin. They cannot control and time their sexual impulses.

Uncontrolled emotions of love and sex are responsible for most of the mental disorders and various forms of insanity. What is unrestrained emotion today may be sex tomorrow. With proper discipline, a person can learn how to transmute their sexual desires to attain purposeful and definite ends. Our sexual desires control much of our emotions and vice-versa. We must learn how to control both of them in order to live successfully.

If you can find the best way to control your sexual desires, you will be among the greatest people in the world. This sexual power is largely misunderstood, but if it is harnessed correctly, you can operate with God-like power. You will have control of almost anything in your field of operation. If you are sexually gifted, you can go even further with your power. However, understand that there will be greater obstacles of temptation because of your sexual gift. This is one of the most challenging areas to have dominion. The more control you have over it, the more personal power will be given to you. Ally yourself with the proper spouse, if necessary, and pool together your resources so that you can build an empire in any area you choose to undertake. The right spouse will be instrumental to your Master Mind and your success. Be sure to use sex and romance correctly to live your dreams. When it comes down to everything, life is about love.

You are the Boss!

Promotion

I am glad that you have had the tremendous pleasure from reading my book. I believe that their strategies can really help refine your authority to propel you toward your future. You will be more successful by knowing how these principles work. I really believe that you are the boss because you can have control over your own life. You can have dominion over your mind and you have the power to choose the opportunities in which you can capitalize on. I truly believe that you have astounding powers within you. Once you realize it, you will have the faith to believe in it.

The power of God can transform your life and give you deep wisdom and understanding over your circumstances. You can walk on a road of excellence when you have a deeper purpose. It all starts with preparation. Now that your mind is prepared, you can handle anything that comes your way. You will need to be Audacious, Contagious, and Tenacious to live a successful life, because many people will not be willing to. Take as many risks as you can and operate with speed and certainty. You must also run as far as you can from conformity and competition. Surround yourself with the right people and learn as much as you could. Always be consistently developing your passions and find a way to enhance your life as well as others. Ask yourself serious questions and be mindful of everything action you take.

You have what you need, now take it to the top. You are now promoted! You have many responsibilities in front of you and improvements that can be made. There is always the call to excellence that demands your attention. Once you can handle the smaller responsibilities in life, you will be given bigger responsibilities. When you learn who you are and what you are made to do, you will conquer everything in your path and nothing will stop you from attaining success. I want you to remember one last thing, YOU ARE THE BOSS! Now it's time to ACT like one…

You Are The Boss!

Top 12 Books

I truly believe that reading can make the difference. Literacy has changed my life forever and I cannot go on a day without reading. It will change your life too. I will list my Top 12 books that changed my life eternally. These books were conducive to my development. It was really challenging to get it down to 12 books because of the hundreds that I have read. You should get them all.

1. **The Holy Bible**-This book led me to a new life I never could have imagined. When I first opened up this book, I was extremely lost and was desperate for change. The words penetrated my heart as I tried to understand the Scriptures. The Holy Bible made me fanatical about reading. It is a compilation of 66 books written by 40 authors. I would suggest you start with the New Testament. I started reading The Gospel of Mark, which is toward the end. I read this book every day because I believe wholeheartedly that it is the Word of God and everything in it can and will be lived out in your life. It has been my greatest teacher. The life of Jesus Christ and other prophets are amazing too! It is the best self-help

book in the world. It is also the best-selling book of all time.

2. **My Utmost for His Highest by Oswald Chambers-**This is a devotional book upon how you can build a stronger relationship with God. Since I have read it, I have been redefined. It gives me spiritual power. I read this book everyday too. It is about character building and teaches you how you can operate without legalism, or 'religiousness.' It is not a religious book, but more like a discovery book. The author is the deepest author I have ever read. He literally talks to you as you read this book. You will question the author, only to find out that he is right. It will really demand you to think deeply. I pray that it will heal you. My Utmost for His Highest is a diamond of a book.

3. **Johnson O'Connor's Vocabulary Builder (1926)**-This book is likened to a dictionary and shows you all kinds of words. Many of them you never even heard of. Bosses know big words. This is a book that I am mastering and it has greatly expanded my command for the English language. It breaks down the history of the words and gives great examples. It is the most classical definitive vocabulary book. Looking up words has never been so

fun! It is very hard to find. You would be missing out if you didn't get it.

4. **Think and Grow Rich by Napoleon Hill-**The title proclaims it all. You want to be rich? That is a perfectly fine thing. It covers how to be rich in all areas, not only spiritually. Think and Grow Rich has created the most self-made millionaires than any other book. It made me a millionaire.

5. **Rich Dad Poor Dad by Robert Kiyosaki-**I would read this book before I read "Think and Grow Rich." It is a beginner's book that will change your whole philosophy about money. It will make you hungry for more. This is one of the most rewarding books that I have read because it has opened up my eyes to the financial world which I did not believe I could explore at the time that I read it. Money is a good thing. Go get it. You are the Boss!

6. **The Wisdom of Andrew Carnegie (as told by Napoleon Hill)**-This book rocked my world. It made me get up and take massive action. I wrote this book because of that book. Andrew Carnegie is my favorite business hero. It is a deep book that touched my soul. It led me to have extraordinary faith. I moved mountain during and after I read this book. You will too.

7. **Success Through a Positive Mental Attitude by Napoleon Hill and W. Clement Stone**-This book explains how you can transcend into the person you want to be. It pushes you to a higher level. Your endurance will increase drastically as you finish this book. You will feel like the champ of the world. It is a easy book and inspiring book to read.

8. **University of Success by Og Mandino**-This book altered my world as well. This is my top 5 book of all-time and I try to recommend it everywhere I go. I found out why I did the things I did by reading this book. I learned how to change my habits by this book. This book is a compilation of Og Mandino's favorite parts of his favorite books. This is the best book, pound-for-pound, in the self-help/success industry. You can get a whole college education from where this book is about to take you when you open it up. Be ready to earn another college degree at the 'University of Success.'

9. **The Magic of Thinking Big by Dr. David Schwartz**-This book cuts right through your heart and shows you how to overcome obstacles. The content of the book is actually bigger than the title is. It is a book that I will read over and over again. There is so much to learn and this

book is very content-rich. He really covers ideas which I could not find in any other book. It is a masterpiece for how small and concise it is.

10. **How to Win Friends and Influence People by Dale Carnegie**-This is a must-read for everyone. Dale Carnegie teaches the simplest methods that can be used to deal with people effectively. The illustrations that are depicted in this book are immaculate. This book will bring you much joy in your life as well as promote you on higher levels of achievement. Handling people is a skill you need to be the boss! It will change your approach and help you get to where you need to be. A life-saving book. I have read it three times already and will read it every year. Also available on audio CD.

11. **Man's Search for Himself by Dr. Rollo May**-This book is quite deep. It is very philosophical and is for the experienced reader. This is the kind of book that will make you think for days. This book shows you how people are and what kind of society we live in. It was written in the 60's, but its precepts are alive today. This book is a must for those who wants to achieve the highest level of thinking.

12. **Pushing to the Front by Orison Swett Marden**-There is great history to this book. Many of the industrialists who

become extremely wealthy read this book. Orison Swett Marden is one of my favorite authors. His prolific mind altered the American scene forever. One day, while he was finishing this the manuscript for this book, his house burned down. The entire manuscript was charred by the fire. Orison Swett Marden started the book all over again. This man is full of heart! You like will change when you see how much blood, sweat, and tears went into this book. Be ready to inhale the truth.

Bonus-One last recommendation that helped me in my development was hearing Earl Nightingale's audio entitled, "**The Strangest Secret.**" This is the best audio program by far and can be found on Youtube.com. For only thirty minutes, Earl Nightingale changed my life forever. He made me want to emulate him and I promise you that this audio piece will change your life. Like I did, he shows you how "You Are the Boss!"

About the Author

Daniel Ally is an award-winning professional speaker and author who pours his heart and soul into his messages. He has a business degree from Penn State University. He is also the author of "The Ultimate Advantage." Daniel Ally is known by many as their expert on leadership and personal development. Daniel's favorite hobbies include exercising, reading, speaking, writing, meeting people, and traveling the world. Daniel's story is the epitome of a rags-to-riches story which he plans to write about in the future. Daniel Ally was born and raised in the inner-city of New York. He now resides in Woodbridge, Virginia. He is a devout follower of Jesus Christ since his life was redeemed on February of 2012.

Made in the USA
Middletown, DE
02 April 2016